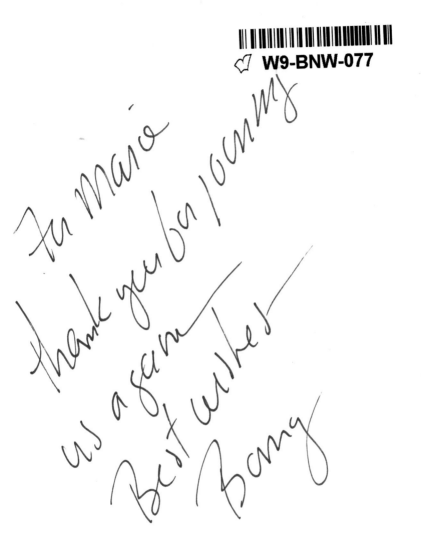

For Mario -
thank you for journey
as a gem
Best wishes
Bonny

Thirty-Three Poems for Mary Lou

The Transforming Power of Love

In Poetry and Prose

❦

by Barry Panter

Sherman Oaks, California

2002

Published by Pavaha Press
14205 Valley Vista Blvd
Sherman Oaks, CA 91423
email: pavahapress@aol.com
Fax (818) 789 9857

Library of Congress
01 126883
ISBN: 0-9712560-4-7
10 9 8 7 6 5 4 3 2 1

Thirty-Three Poems
for Mary Lou

❦

The Transforming Power of Love

in Poetry and Prose

by Barry Panter

Sherman Oaks, California

2002

I was blessed to be married to Mary Lou
for thirty-three years. For those of you who knew
her—with these poems you will know her better.
For those of you who didn't know her—let the
poems introduce her to you.
I read some of them to her during the weeks
and months before she died.
I wanted her to know not only how much
I love her, but also how grateful I am to her—
how her love and vitality and Spirit
transformed and enriched my life.
I offer these poems now to you—
that her Loving Spirit may enrich your life too.

Mary Lou—My Dearest, Sweet Mary Lou.
I fell head over heels in love with you
the moment I first saw you.
And I have been in love with you ever since—
for your kindness,
your gentleness,
your understanding.
You are the best wife to me I could possibly imagine.
Thank you for thirty-three years of our marriage—
for Amy, Adrienne and David,
for the wonderful travels we've enjoyed,
for loving me through our troubles
as well as our joys.
I love you more today
than I did on the day we were married,
for you have taught me life's greatest lesson—
You taught me how to love—
and I will love you always, Darling.

Forever yours, Barry

I thought I fell in love with you
because of the beauty of your face and figure,
   and the great times we had together.
But since you're so sick
   and illness has taken so much away,
I realize now what I barely grasped before—
I fell in love with you for the beauty of your Spirit,
   and that beauty shines through everything.

It hovers around you as an aura.
Your Spirit shines through your illness.
It shines through your pain and suffering.
It shines through this terrible ordeal.
Your kindness, your gentleness,
   your loving, giving, graceful Spirit
     shines through everything.
You have never been more beautiful to me, Darling.
I love you, and I always will.

    Yours Forever, Barry

Remember, Darling—
Standing on the deck of a Chinese Junk,
the Hong Kong Harbor;
Your hair blowing in the gentle breeze,
Your eyes sparkling against the
just before twilight darkening blue sky,
My twenty-five-year-old bride.
Your beautiful face—
filled with happiness,
filled with love,
filled with the promise of our future together.
That moment is in my heart forever.
I close my eyes—as I close yours—
I see you there.

I smell the sweet, gentle softness of you.
Your Spirit envelops me.
I can feel your love.
My Darling,
I will love you forever.
I am yours forever.

You gave yourself to me,
    No shyness, no hesitation.
I was seeking sex—
    You surprised me and confused me—
        You gave me—Love!
How long did it take for me to know the difference?
Five years? Ten years? of your unwavering love,
    without complaint
        without demand—
    Until it seeped into me,
        Infused me with its warmth,
            Merged into my Being,
And opened my heart
    and my eyes
        to a new world.

You preferred to stay in the background,
fearful of the light,
Yet smoothing the way,
encouraged me to step into it.
I ran the race.
I heard the cheers.
I grasped the prize.
But, my Darling,
I need your smile at the race well run.
I need your heart to race with mine.
I need to lay the laurel at your feet.
My love...my heart...
What is my life without you?

Thirty three years,
Three children.
I've tried to give you the world,
 And we've had our share.
But it's the simple pleasures that meant the most to you.
 The children
 The children
 The children.
Bathing them,
 Reading to them,
  Brushing their hair,
   Playing with them,
    Singing to them.
Stroking Negra, Mignon at your feet.
Roses,
 Daffodils,
  Crocuses!
Reaching out, filling everyone with your love.
My God! My Love, how you gave of yourself!

Remember, Darling,
Our first Opera together—

> *The Vienna Opera House, standing room only,*
> *Madame Butterfly silhouetted against the night sky.*

You were thrilled.
  We were thrilled.
    We were hooked!
Opera Opera Everywhere—
  Mozart
    Lucia in Naples
      Carmen in Paris
—You drank it in like a parched flower.
And Vienna—the music, the strudel, the schlage!!
Oh, Darling—
  Your energy,
    Your excitement!
      To see you striding through life with giant steps,
        Gulping it all in, blossoming.
And now…now that you're leaving, your energy waning—
Oh, Sweetheart—to see you dying—Can I bear it?
Will I ever listen to Puccini or Pachelbel again
          …without crying?
  I don't know.

So many years of loving you and being loved by you.
Your love is the alchemist.

　The doubts are gone,

　　uncertainty is gone.

In their place

　The confidence you gave me.

Your love, your faith, your unwavering belief in me,

　have made me strong.

I only wish I had strength enough to help you, Darling—

　to tear this sickness from your throat,

　　to make you whole again,

　　　to give you back your strength,

　　　　your vitality, your delight in little things,

　　　　to see your beauty return to you.

My Darling…I love you so. Don't leave me.
Please, don't leave me now.

My Love,
Your love has healed me,
   subdued the anger
      released the resentment.
So many years of your constant, unwavering,
   forgiving, accepting Love—
Your magnificent astounding wonderful gift to me.
If only I could return the gift.
If only my love could pour into you,
Into every crevice and fissure in your body and your soul,
To heal your aches and soothe your pains.
My Darling, know that I understand
   the magnificence,
    the wonder,
        the amazing power of your love.

Dad was trying to make the best of it—
*   A shiksa for his son.*
But it went against his every grain.
I thought he might sit Shiva for me.
I was prepared for that—
You were worth it.
But he took a deep breath…
*   and said, "Hello, Mary Lou".*
I think he first started to love you
*   at the all-you-can-eat lobster dinner—*
He'd never seen a Michigan farm girl in action.

Nothing was safe—
*   Not the claws, not the feet,*
*   not the littlest hidden-away sliver of meat*
*   could escape your attack.*
*   Never mind the utensils*
*   Never mind the manners—*
*   This was passion!*
And he loved you for it.

And then the girls' noses—
At first he merely said, "What lovely shapes they have."
And then, "They look a little like me."
And finally, proudly, "They get their noses
from my side of the family, you know."
You won his heart too, Sweetheart.
No lobster morsel safe from your onslaught—
No heart hardened enough to withstand your smile.

Roses, Daffodils, Crocuses, Poppies —
All the bright cheerful ones, so like you —
Strewn everywhere;

  the yard, the kitchen, the family room.
The colors, the scent — everywhere.
Above all else, the children.
The children — with a special place for babies —
  "freshest from the hand of God."
And the animals —
 Whatever walked, whatever squawked,
   whatever swam;
  All the pets over all the years.
The dogs, the cats, and bunnies and chickens,
 ducks and hamsters, and even Shasta, our pony.
In that way, you never left the farm.
And the last two —
 Mignon, who followed you around
  like the little puppy she once was;
 And Negra, always in your lap
  purring her contented purr as you stroked her back.
You spoke their language, Darling.
They loved you too.

I look at your watercolors and I see you in them.
Five bright yellow poppies against a field of blue
        rising from slender stalks of green.
Did you know the magic of the number?
    The five of us—
        Amy, Adrienne, David, you and I—
            united forever in your heart and work.
Your work—family, home, art, children, flowers, pets.
Strewing love with every word,
    Every glance, Every act,
        until like a tidal wave it overcame everything—
            overcame doubts, anger, resentment, fear—
All fell before the power of your love.

It meant so much to Frank—
He loved your rum cake.
You rose from bed to make it.
Yet, that's who you are.
But then, how many are allowed
        to celebrate ninety years?
And how many are there like you?
Doing, giving, baking, painting, planting—
Pouring your love in so many ways into so many lives.
How many lives have been changed—like mine—
    by your love?
I'll count the stars...

To see you struggling for your every breath,
Your body swollen—the body I've held so many times.
So many times you've given yourself to me,
        such pleasure over so many years.
Oh, my Darling—
    Do you know I'm here?
        Are you there?
Your swollen eyes,
    no flicker of awareness.
Come back—come back, my love!
Let me hold you again.
Let me make love to you again.
Remember how our bodies danced
        and our hearts sang—
Oh, my Darling—my Darling...

Red drops falling slowly through glass,
        like my tears...
Sometimes they fall—
        I don't even know they're there,
                until I feel them rolling down my cheeks.
My Darling—Is it over?
Just the machine pushing air in and out,
    the tubes dripping dripping dripping,
        trying for another miracle.
I want to crawl in bed with you,
To hold you in my arms one last time,
To tell you softly again and again,
    I love you...I love you...
        I will always love you.

Do they only hire angels to work in hospitals?
Or do the aides and nurses become angels
after working there awhile?
So many acts of kindness,
So much tenderness and caring.
I've seen them gently wipe your brow
as tenderly as you wiped our children after baths;
Rubbing cream into your back
to ease your pain.
Where do they come from,
with such tender hands
and gentle hearts
and patient minds?
Are they Michigan farm girls like you?
Bathed in love by adoring parents?
Are they too
oldest daughters helping over-worked moms
tend too many kids?

You—above all—deserve their care.
You who have cared and tended and given
    Without end
        Without complaint
            With only kindness and love,
Always with love.
It's your turn, Darling—
        Take their love
        Take my love
        Take all our love.
Let it flow into you like a healing river,
        Into your body
            your being
                your soul.
Come back to me, my Darling
Please...Come back to me.
I love you so...

Perhaps it's because your work is done—
So many years of giving…
    You were radiant in your love,
        Happiest in the acts of giving.
You've done your work so well, Sweetheart—
            Three strong children,
            A husband transformed.
I think you were at your happiest
                whenever you held a baby,
        Gently cooing and enfolding that gift
            into your arms.
They all loved you. They all responded to you.
Thank you for your gifts to me,
    For the many years of our love.
I guess it's your time…
It breaks my heart to see you go.
Perhaps it's time.
    Goodbye, my love…
        goodbye.
I love you. I love you. I will always love you.

I marveled at you as Mother—
All the kids in the neighborhood were at our house.
Johnny, Corinne, Mia, Vanessa, Tracy, Philip, Ian, Ronnie...
It wasn't just the ice cream and chocolate chip pancakes
in Mickey Mouse head shapes,
and the arts and the crafts,
and the games, and the adventures.
It was you, Darling—
no judgements
no criticism
no hurt feelings,
But quiet acceptance—
Holding when they needed holding,
Kissing the bruises when they needed kissing.
I've never heard you tell me or others what to do—
No instructions about love or kindness, or generosity.
You lived it—you just lived it.
And the children knew.
They knew what they needed to make them strong,
to make them whole.
So they came to you
to be sheltered
to be nurtured
to be loved.

I can't keep things straight—

> *When did you start to get sick again?*
> *What day did you go back in the hospital?*
> *When did I return?*

When was the last time I heard you say, I love you?
  And I to you?
When did your mind start to drift?
When was the last moment we spoke to each other
        and saw each other's Soul?
I can't keep it straight in my mind.
Oh, my Darling—
  I don't want to know these things.
    I don't want to know...

Your faults?
So few, so very few.
Do they matter?
   They hardly move the scales
      when weighed against your overflowing heart—
         cascading, pouring like a gigantic river
            into our lives.
So many lives...
   touched, transformed, made whole
      by the power of your love.

Whose words are these?
Where do they come from?
They form in me—words, phrases—
*   as I sit by your side,*
*   as I drive to be with you,*
*   as I sit and look at your picture,*
*   From our love for each other,*
A gift from God, a final soothing gift for you.
May they comfort you, my Darling,
*   as you travel on your way.*

Oh, My God!
Sweetheart, Wake Up!
You look like you could—
You look like you're just sleeping
Oh—I love you, Darling.
But you are cold;
Your skin is cold.
Let me stroke your hair.
Did you move your eyes?
Did they just flutter?
I'll just sit here with you for awhile...
Did your chest just move?
I swear it did.
Can I bear this pain?
Can I survive without you?
Easier perhaps to join you.
I want to be with you.
I feel faint.
I'll just lie down here
  next to you for awhile.

I never thought when I bought this jacket
*   that I'd be wearing it to your funeral.*
I only thought how glad you'd be for me to have it.
But then—that's who you are—
*   always for me,*
*   always for the girls,*
*   always for David.*
I guess I knew, my Darling—I guess I knew.

I never thought when I bought this table
*   that I'd be laying your pictures out upon it*
*   for everyone to see.*
I only thought how much you'd like it,
*   so pretty in its place.*
I guess I knew

I never thought when redoing the garden
*   that you'd see it for so brief a time.*
I only thought how much it would please you,
*   your favorite flowers everywhere.*
I guess I knew —I guess I knew.

A yellow rose upon your casket,
   slowly, slowly,
      into the ground.
My heart goes with you, Darling.
  My heart goes with you
    into the grave.
My arms are heavy.
So tired...
  I feel so tired.
So old...
  I feel so terribly old.

Did you know how many people love you?
Not just Amy Adrienne David and me.
Our friends—so many friends—
       Calling with tears.
I can hear the pain in their hearts,
So many friends from so many places...

The aides, the nurses, the doctors—
I'm sure they know,
       "Don't care too much—
             It'll tear your heart out."
But they cared for you, Sweetheart.
They call—they cry.
They too
       couldn't hold themselves back from you.

Yen and Susan, Mariella, Mavay, Pia,
Roberto, Claudia, Shauna, Jeri.
They didn't just help you
with the house and garden,
your nails and hair.
They knew — They knew you.
They recognized your Spirit.
They were warmed by your glow.
They were happy in your smile.

The calls, the flowers,
The love that is their bond with you,
flowing back to you —
You who have sent it out
to so many for so many years.
They loved you back and were the better for it.
I can feel its force as it flows back toward you.
Oh, Sweetheart — so much love for you!

You embraced my family,
Opened your heart and held them to it.
"Whither thou goest, I will go."
      You lived it, Darling.
Mom and Dad, Aunt Dorothy,
  Aunt Kathryn, Aunt Emma,
      Uncle Harry, Freddie, Harmon—
You are side by side with them now.
My place is ready beside you, Sweetheart.
I'll be with you soon.

Is this how it goes?
The family, the friends,
the pictures, the memories.
Holding on to you a little while longer,
Trying to not let you go...
Oh, my Darling...my Darling...my Darling.

How many days, weeks, months, years
  before the pain begins to go?
No hurry, my Darling.
Grief is not unwelcomed,
It is an affirmation of our love.
Feeling the pain—I'm with you.
You are here with me—
  my life...slowing down
    ...walking slowly with you awhile
      ...with you in my heart.

Everyone is so kind,
  stopping by,
    talking...sharing...giving
      the flowers, the food...
Sharing their memories,
Sharing their love for you.

She's gone, Mignon—she's gone.
Don't go running so eagerly into the bedroom—
     She's not there.
Don't wander around the house, your face so sad—
     She's gone.
No more her gentle hand upon your back.
     No more her softness,
          her warmth next to you in bed.
Never know again her touch, her caress.
She's gone Mignon—
     She's gone.

I reach for you
        in the night,
    to touch again your softness,
        to feel your warmth.
God's gift—two loving hearts.
I reach for you in the darkness,
            forgetting—you're not there,
            forgetting that you're gone.

It would have made you so happy
    to see Adrienne in her wedding dress.
Radiant, just like you.
Oh, Darling—
        the wedding,
        the grandchildren,
        so many wonderful times—
What will they be without you?
Will I smile again?
Will I ever know again what we've known—
        The happiness
        the joy
        the excitement of you.

I'll never understand—nor do I need to
Why you took her when you did—
One of your most beautiful children,
   Fair of face,
      Fair of body.
Yet they paled
         compared to the goodness of her soul
         and the love that radiated from her.
The light from within was your Light, O Lord.
You took her physical beauty,
But you left her Spirit and her Love.
I close my eyes.
   I see her smile.
      I feel her next to me.
         I'm enfolded in her love.
My God, my God—
Schema Yisroal Adonai elohanu Adonai elhud.
Blessed art Thou O Lord our God
King of the Universe.
Thank you for the time we shared.
   Thank you for the love we knew.
      ...Thy will be done.

We had been preparing to go to New York for a vacation when she became ill. She had pain in her stomach and fever. She went into the hospital on September 15th and that night went into shock. Emergency surgery led to removal of four feet of gangrenous bowel. An artery to her bowel had become obstructed. She was in the hospital nearly five months. There were so many complications: five surgeries, fever, a severe allergic reaction, adrenal insufficiency, pulmonary emboli, jaundice, and terrible painful rashes. So many procedures—hundreds and hundreds of needles, intubations, skin biopsy, liver biopsy—on and on. Yet she never complained. She'd cry from time to time. But when she wasn't in pain or totally exhausted, she was cheerful—giving her Spirit, her charm, to brighten everyone's life—seemingly not a special effort for her. That's who she was.

She came home on February 7th. We went to a few movies, and out to dinner occasionally. She was up and about the house. When she sat, Negra was on her lap, Mignon at her feet—until April 4th when she developed a fever. The next day it was 105.3 and she was back in the hospital. Her adrenals were exhausted, her electrolytes were off. She was treated for an infection and then for shock. She had difficulty breathing. Her body started to swell with the fluids being given intravenously. She was alert at first. We spoke. She talked to the children. We told her how much we loved her. As her condition worsened, she became confused and then her mind just drifted off. All the efforts of her doctors and nurses and aides were not enough.

A few hours before she died, Adrienne read some of her favorite lines from *The Highwayman* to her...

> *"The moon was a ghostly galleon*
> *tossed upon cloudy seas.*
> *And the Highwayman came riding, riding, riding.*
> *The Highwayman came riding."*

Pachelbel's *Canon*—her favorite—was playing over and over again. She died a few minutes before midnight on April 14th.

I miss you,
  Especially in the evening
  when the house is quiet,
  while I sit with Mignon and Negra
  listening to the floor creaking.

I miss you when I go to bed—
  your goodnight kiss,
  your soft warm body curled next to mine.
  I miss holding you.

I miss you in the night
  when I reach for you.
  I miss slowly running my hand
  from your buttock to your knee
  along your silky, so smooth soft skin.

I miss you at Christmas time...
  You so loved Christmas,
  Buying presents all year long.
  I found the blouse you bought for Amy
  and the shirts for David,
  Presents from you—for Christmases to come.

I miss you when I watch the sunset,
  the quiet moments we shared,
  sometimes with pensive conversation,
  sometimes just sharing the silence.

I miss taking your hand.
I miss your touch.
I miss your smile.
My darling, I miss you every day of my life...

The pain is leaving.
In its place—
            Comforting, cherished memories,
            stored treasures from our past.
The soothing memories of you,
            another of your many gifts to me,
            easing my pain,
healing my torn and wounded heart.

I witnessed Mary Lou's Life.

This is my testimony.

Mary Lou—My dearest, sweet Mary Lou. I fell head over heels in love with you the moment I first saw you.

I was late. Grand rounds had already started. Dr. Kagan and the pediatric residents and interns had seen the first two patients and were on the third patient down the hospital corridor. The charge nurse at the nurses' station motioned me to hurry and join rounds.

As I started to go, I saw Mary Lou in the isolation room behind the station. She was wearing a cap and gown and a mask covering all of her face except her eyes. She was holding her patient, a little three-year-old girl, in her arms.

I didn't know at the time why I was so attracted to her, so instantly. I could hardly see much behind her cap and mask and gown. But I felt it— that instantaneous magical life-asserting impulse-forcing attraction. I knew I had to meet her, to talk to her. I wanted to know who she was, what she looked like—everything about her.

I've read about falling in love at first sight, and I believe in it. I experienced it full force. We know so much at that first glance, most of it unconsciously. We know it with our hearts, not with our minds. In love, I'll trust the heart every time.

I joined grand rounds and when we finished about two hours later, I went back to Mary Lou. To enter the isolation room, I had to go through the entire routine—donning mask and gown, putting on gloves—and when I had completed it all and was in the room, I turned to Mary Lou and said, "This isn't a professional visit. This is a social call. Will you have dinner with me tonight?"

She didn't exactly faint from the shock, but her eyes opened wide and I could see the surprise in them above the mask.

I didn't know until later that her mother had warned her about men like me. Mary Lou had grown up on a farm in Michigan. They were Baptists—God-fearing, fundamentalist, fire-and-brimstone, God-is-everywhere, He-sees-everything-you-do Baptists. When she left home to go to nursing school in Chicago, her mother had warned her to be a good girl, to stay out of trouble, and to watch out for those big city boys.

After finishing her training and heading to Cedars of Lebanon Hospital in Hollywood, her mother's warnings became even stronger. Now, here she was, confronted—so she thought—by exactly what her mother had warned her of—one of those Hollywood swingers.

She turned me down. I was crushed. I felt the blood drain out of me. I slunk from the isolation room like the snake she must have thought I was.

Later that day, as I was writing an order on one of the charts at the nurses' station, I felt a gentle tap on my shoulder. There she was, without the mask and gown—and she was beautiful! She said, "I can go out tomorrow night if you like." If I like? If I like? I went from feeling crushed flat on the floor to flying above the moon—I was ecstatic!

What was it about her? Was this the Madonna that I had longed for as a lonely child, for all of my life up until then? Earlier, in the isolation room, the little girl had been curled so trustingly, so gently into her arms. Did I unconsciously see myself in the same place, held securely by her? I wasn't aware of it at the time. I have thought about that first moment many times since.

❧

My mother was severely depressed a number of times during my childhood and even later. From the time I was an infant, it was my "assignment" to be with my mother, to take care of her, to comfort her, and finally to heal her. I am grateful that she lived long enough for me to become a doctor, first a pediatrician and then a psychiatrist, so that I could finally, with the help of the anti-depressants that became available, play a role in her recovery. She lived her final twenty years without the severe debilitating depressions that had previously caused her to plead with me for death.

I remember, as a child of eight or nine years, being home alone with her as she cried in her locked bedroom. "My lifetime is sorrow. Help me die."

All I could do was cry and sit on the floor on the other side of the door and wonder if she would be alive when the door finally was opened.

My mother suffered terribly. The depressions came every two or three years and lasted many months. My father was busy with his business, sometimes working two jobs to support us, and didn't know what to do for her.

When I was three or four years old, she and I took a train trip from our home in New Jersey to California to be with Aunt Dorothy, my mother's sister. That was Dad's response to Mom's depressions—send her to Dorothy.

It was actually a good plan—Dorothy was one of the angels in this world. She and Mom sat for hours and talked. I remember them walking on Las Rosas Lane in Santa Barbara, hand in hand. After a few months, Mom felt better and we returned to New Jersey.

I don't remember much about the train trip to California except that it seemed to last forever. I don't remember her talking with me—I think she just sat in the compartment, silent in her depression. I walked up and down the train, from one end to the other, over and over again. My feelings of loneliness and sadness were overwhelming. The trip must have taken three or four days. I only have memories of my mother sitting quietly, and of my walking from one end of the train to the other, back and forth, over and over again.

Was I yearning for my mother to hold me? To caress me? To love me? I don't remember thinking or feeling those needs. Did all of this flash through my mind when I saw Mary Lou holding the little girl? No, it didn't. I only knew, felt, was impelled, was pushed by a force beyond my understanding—I had to meet her.

❧

Our first date almost never happened. I went to pick her up at her apartment at seven o'clock and knocked on the door. No answer. I waited ten minutes, fifteen minutes, twenty minutes. It was one of those apartment buildings that are so common in Southern California—a pool in the center, and the apartments in one or two stories built around it. I was walking out of the building when I saw her hurrying into her apartment to get ready.

I think that if I had left a minute earlier, or if she had been a few minutes later, it was possible that we might have never gone out. For all my bravado, I was insecure, and I think I might have been so hurt by being stood up that I would have lacked the courage to ask her out again. Was it good fortune? Was it fate? Was it is our destiny?

We went out for a sandwich and it must have been three or four hours that we just sat talking. We talked and talked and talked. I remember looking at her, staring at her, and thinking over and over again—*My God, she's so beautiful! She is unbelievably beautiful.*

I didn't think about whether I was in love or not— the question didn't really enter my mind. I just knew that I wanted to be with her. From the moment I first saw her, I never dated anyone else.

Before we met, I had been going out with a number of girls, mostly trying to get them to bed with me, with very little success. I didn't know much about good relationships. Because of my mother's depression and the fact that she was emotionally unavailable to me, I didn't trust women. I didn't count on them to be constant and laughing and true. I also had a great deal of anger and was driven by that and my hormones. I wanted to use the girls I was dating. I wanted to control and dominate them, and maybe then they wouldn't leave me. Or I would leave them before they left me, and hurt them in the process, as I had been hurt. I was not a nice person. I was selfish and didn't know how to trust. I didn't know how to give much of myself. I didn't know how to love.

How could all of this change? I was in psychoanalysis for ten years. It helped, but it was Mary Lou's love that made the difference. She loved me quietly, fully, determinedly, patiently, constantly, undemandingly, adoringly, year after year after year. Love was the healer. Mary Lou's love healed me and nourished my soul. She gave me exactly what I needed. I am so blessed that this girl came out of the farmlands of Michigan and came into my life and loved me. She loved me with a love I never knew existed, loved me with all her heart, and gave to me, and healed me, and filled in so many of the empty spaces in my heart and my soul.

❧

We went bowling for our fourth date. Mary Lou was not athletic, but she was willing to try almost anything, especially if I suggested it. When we returned to her apartment, she asked if I would like some potetsa. I had no idea what it was but I was so infatuated that I would say yes to anything she suggested. She explained that it was a holiday bread for special occasions that her mother had taught her to make. I knew what I wanted the special occasion to be!

As she went about the preparations in the kitchen, I went about my preparations in the living room. Setting the stage for seduction, I carefully arranged pillows and put on romantic music. In my eagerness, I had my scene ready within fifteen minutes.

What I didn't know was that making potetsa from scratch takes a very very long time. And that time can double or triple when the hope and anticipation for sex is on one's mind. Mary Lou was busily making noises with a rolling pin, bread mold, pots and pans, singing all the while.

I didn't realize until much later in our relationship that one of Mary Lou's underlying beliefs was that you should work hard for the person you care about. It is how you demonstrate your love. Growing up as the oldest child in a family of seven plus three foster children means there is a lot of work to do, and Mary Lou did a lot of it.

That night, I think it took three or four hours until she came out of the kitchen proudly holding a plate of freshly baked potetsa in her hands. By then, I'd given up any hope of action. When I saw her coming out of the kitchen, holding the freshly baked bread, offering it to me so openly, so honestly, so lovingly, I realized that she was offering me something so much more valuable than the bread, so much more wonderful than her body. I felt that she was holding out her heart to me, offering her love on a plain porcelain plate that she had carefully brought with her from the plains of lower Michigan. It was the best bread I have ever eaten.

You give yourself to me —
no shyness no hesitation.

On our fifth or sixth date, when we returned to Mary Lou's apartment, making potetsa was not on our agenda. I didn't think of whether I was committed to her or not, but I just wasn't interested in being with anyone else. Mary Lou was on my mind day and night, only Mary Lou. She, though, had made a more conscious decision and commitment to me. She didn't say or ask me for anything or hint in any way about a commitment, but I think she thought of us as a couple and that we were to be together.

On that date, I didn't have to wait for her to finish working in the kitchen. We sat down on the sofa and soon our feelings for each other had taken over. We were kissing and hugging and touching and gasping. The passion that had been implied in our togetherness had sprung to life. No longer implied, it was in action, and soon we were making love. I remember that evening and that time so clearly. She wasn't shy. She wasn't hesitant. She was ready. We had such pleasure in each other. Her skin was so soft—For all of her life, she had the softest silkiest skin.

What I didn't realize during those first bliss-filled moments was that we were unconsciously pledging ourselves to each other. Our lovemaking was our unspoken commitment to each other—to hold, to cherish, to love—for a lifetime.

I wish I could say that I knew I loved her that night and that our lovemaking was an expression of my conscious feeling for her, but the baggage I carried with me prevented that awareness. This was 1965, and I thought nice girls didn't do this until they were married. I desired her and could hardly keep my hands off her. I looked forward to seeing her in the hospital and speaking to her and to being with her as much as possible. But I also remember thinking after we made love that first time that it was too soon. I wished that she had waited or made me wait longer.

What I didn't know was that Mary Lou was not just having sex—She was expressing her love for me. It was as natural and timely as a rose opening in the sun, blooming when it is time to bloom. It was time to give ourselves, time to know the intense indescribable pleasure of making love to each other.

I soon got over the feelings I had that this was too early or wrong, or we shouldn't be doing this. A great help was the fact that we were young and in love, and had unbridled hormones. And our loving—the sex—was truly "making love". Our love for each other was increasing as naturally and forcefully as the sun rises over a calm lake. We were spending most nights together at my apartment, and only occasionally would she spend the night at hers. She had a roommate and felt that she should spend some time with her.

For us, "making love" was literally true—It was part of creating our love. Our physical desires—the pleasure we found in each other, our lust, and passion—all were the flames that fired us and forged a love that bound us together. It was a love that kept expanding, that nourished and enriched us, and lifted us to a realm of joy that I had never even dreamt of before I knew and loved and was loved by Mary Lou.

About a month after we started dating, I went to Philadelphia for a pediatric convention and then on to New Jersey to visit my parents and brother and sister-in-law. The last thing my father said to me as I was getting on the plane to return to Los Angeles was, "Barry, whatever you do, don't marry a shiksa."

I was hurt. I was angry. It wasn't because I was thinking of getting married, but because I didn't like my father telling me how to live my life. His philosophy of "stick with your own kind" never made sense to me, but I understand why he felt that way.

He was born in Eastern Europe—Poland or Russia, depending on who had won the last battle. His little village of Vilna Geberna was often raided and plundered by the Cossacks, and the women were raped. His earliest memory was as a five-year-old, when Cossacks thundered into the village on their horses. All the Jews tried to scatter and run. One of the soldiers on horseback drew his sword and beheaded a woman. The boy who became my father saw her head fall off and roll down the street before him. I never shared his need to segregate with fellow Jews, but I never blamed him for his feelings.

When I returned from Philadelphia, Mary Lou had a surprise for me—She had moved into my apartment! We hadn't talked about living together or where our relationship was headed. We were just enjoying it and each other. But there she was—Her dresses and her uniforms were in the closet, her shoes neatly stacked next to mine. Even her potetsa-making utensils were in the tiny kitchen.

I was surprised and happy that she had moved in, and also curious. She explained that her roommate had moved out, leaving her with all of the rent to pay. It was too expensive by herself so she decided to move in with me. I asked about her lease. She admitted that she packed everything up in the middle of the night, loaded it into her car, and drove to my place. She asked if that was OK with me.

Of course it was OK. It was better than OK—It was fabulous. We could spend even more time together. Neither one of us had to drive back and forth from one apartment to the other. It seemed so natural, so comfortable. Nothing was being planned—It was just happening. Everything was unfolding as it seemed it should.

Mary Lou was an excellent cook. She could make just about anything she set her mind to, not just potetsa. I could boil water and fry eggs. But one of those first nights together in my apartment, I decided to impress her with my cooking—and, of course, go to bed with her as soon after dinner as possible.

We had steak, which Mary Lou tactfully prevented me from turning into shoe leather. My pièce de résistance—the grand finale, the ultimate seducer—was to be bananas flambé. I carefully peeled the bananas and ladled nearly half a bottle of brandy over them, and then, trying to be as suave as Cary Grant, I lit the match and held it to the brandy. Nothing happened. The brandy was supposed to burst into the soft bluish-rose-colored flame and tenderly envelop the bananas, all of which would be a powerful aphrodisiac. I lit another match. Still nothing. My planned seduction was quickly turning into a bumbling disaster.

Mary Lou gently suggested that heating the brandy might work. Brilliant! I followed her advice and voila! —The flames roared to life, and the bananas were engulfed. They were as potent an aphrodisiac as I had hoped, and the night was another of so many wonderful nights over so many years of love and passion and holding and caring and giving with my darling, with my love, my sweetheart, my sweet Mary Lou.

We continued living together, loving together, for a year or probably longer. I finished my pediatric residency but didn't feel ready to open my own practice or go into an established one, so I did locum tenens.

One of the pediatricians on staff at the hospital knew I had no plans after the residency and asked if I would cover his practice for several weeks while he went on vacation. I was glad to do it. It was a wonderful arrangement for everyone. He paid me half of the gross billings, a fortune after an intern's salary of $55.28 (plus meals) every two weeks, and he could go away and have his office expenses covered.

Soon other pediatricians heard that I was available, and I had as much work as I wanted. I'd work for two or three weeks and then take off for one or two weeks. Mary Lou was doing special-duty nursing so she too could work or not as she wished. We would work for a few weeks and then just be home or go on a vacation. We went to Hawaii for sun and Mammoth Mountain to ski, and other great destinations. We were living a marvelous life together.

We never talked about getting married or where our relationship was going. We were just enjoying it, loving it, and loving each other. I didn't try to guess what was going on in her mind about us. And even though I was in psychoanalysis, I wasn't reflecting on where we were headed, but something was bubbling beneath the surface. At some time in the fall of 1966, I casually asked her what she thought of getting married in the spring.

I wish that I had gotten down on my knee and looked longingly and hopefully into that beautiful face of the girl I loved and pleaded with her to marry me. I wish I had told her I couldn't live without her, that I wanted to be with her for the rest of my life. But all I did was casually, offhandedly mention it over my shoulder while doing dishes in our apartment after dinner.

Mary Lou's reaction wasn't the movie version either. She did not fall into my arms and declare passionately, "Yes, YES, of course, my darling. I'm yours—forever yours."

What happened was more of a panic reaction. I think she suddenly envisioned going from our idyllic lifestyle of work and vacation and love and loving and relaxation to taking care of nine kids, constantly doing dishes and laundry and cooking and changing diapers. And she got scared.

The few times previously when we mentioned anything about marriage, I had said something that I probably heard in a Woody Allen movie about not making any major decisions until I was finished with my analysis. Does a person want to avoid falling in love, committing heart and life to an angel, moving forward in life? No, life doesn't stand still—It can't stand still.

Although I was surprised by her reaction, I wasn't worried or upset by it. I knew I loved her, and I knew she loved me. I knew we belonged together, so I suggested what any psychoanalyst-to-be would, that she see a psychiatrist and talk this over.

And she did. Mary Lou saw a wonderful, wise, warm-hearted, loving psychiatrist. I have had the good fortune to know several such people over the years. It is one of the reasons I wanted to be a psychoanalyst. I liked what I saw in some analysts who had been in practice a long time. When one hears so many life stories—the tragedies, the hopes and dreams, the losses and rebirths—they can help to form a compassionate, kind and wise person.

Unfortunately, over the years, I have also seen hearts that have turned to stone—professionals who were only interested in abiding by the rules rather than listening to and understanding the needs of the heart. Those hearts are sometimes sad and sinking, belonging to individuals who turn to them for help, often as a last resort, in desperation. Help starts with kindness and acceptance and compassion. Without these, the understanding and explaining are almost worthless.

Mary Lou saw Bertram Spira. He listened to her story, and gently discussed her fears with her. She came to understand more of what she was afraid of. She looked at and understood and faced the dragons that she had feared would eat her up, and, as often happens, they began to disappear.

She realized that a life with our own family, of children, would be a different life than that of her parents. Thank you, Dr. Spira. Thank you for your kindness, for your understanding. Thank you for helping Mary Lou and me create the life we did.

While Mary Lou was seeing Dr. Spira, I was also doing what I could to persuade her to marry me. Once the idea had emerged into consciousness for me and even passed from my lips to her ears, the soft flame of "Let's get married in the spring" became a bonfire in my heart. I was aflame with the hope and dream and desire to marry her.

I'm not sure how the idea for our honeymoon emerged. I didn't consciously think of making her an offer she couldn't refuse, and I don't remember her mentioning it. I knew she loved to travel. I knew of her wish to go beyond her ken, and of her mother's instructions to do so. As casually as I had asked her to marry me, I suggested that we buy two around-the-world airline tickets, take all the money we had, and just keep traveling until the money ran out. That did it! It was the offer she couldn't refuse. Soon we were planning our wedding.

❧

A shiksa for his son.
But it went against his every grain.
I thought he might sit shiva for me.
I was prepared for that. You were worth it.

My father—What to do about my father? What would my father do? Of course I was worried, but I had made my decision. My father wasn't thrilled, but despite his warning to me, he took a deep breath and said hello to Mary Lou.

He was never rude or unkind to her, but in the beginning, he just couldn't be warm or friendly or happy. Mary Lou wouldn't allow herself to show any hurt, any unfriendliness. Her nature was always to be outgoing and accepting of others, and to overlook their faults and unkindness. She continued to be her natural self. Her warmth, her love, her kindness in the face of my father's initial coolness and unhappiness, finally won his heart.

No lobster morsel safe from your onslaught.
No heart hardened enough to withstand your smile.

Actually, Mary Lou had a good relationship with my father before I did. When I was a boy, my father was always working and had little time for my brother and me. I thought he just didn't like me or want to spend any time with me. He was very critical, not only of me and everything I did when he was around, but he also criticized my mother and my brother. I was often hurt and, even more often, angry with him.

Yes, I would have been hurt if he sat shiva for me,

the Hebrew prayer for the dead. Sometimes a father who disapproves of the behavior of a son, sits shiva for him and considers him dead ever after. But had that occurred, I would have returned that with anger and then acceptance of my loss. Nothing was going to stop me from marrying Mary Lou.

❧

Are you ready?

In love, you have to be ready to risk everything.
When you hear the knock on the door—
When you feel the tap on your shoulder—
When you are struck by Cupid's arrow—

If Mary Lou had been afraid of
*   "the big city guy"...*
If I had been too hurt by her initial rejection...
If she had been another five minutes late...
If I had been afraid of my father sitting Shiva
*   and considering me dead...*
When you feel that moment of shock
*   as Cupid's arrow hits,*
Are you ready?

It is amazing to me how often I have realized and have heard in the lives of my patients, that parents—well-meaning parents, seemingly acting out of their love and the desire for their children to be happy—give advice and make harsh demands or threats to them. And in almost every instance, the child—even a young child—knows better what is best for him or her. We all know in our hearts what we need. We know what is good for us, far better than anyone else knows—better than parents, better than teachers, better than analysts. All that we should do is take from them their wisdom, consider their opinions and advice, and then look into our own hearts and follow that internal wisdom. If we don't do that—if we allow ourselves to be threatened into submission, or if we give up on what we know in our hearts to be true—what have we done? We have betrayed ourselves. We have been beaten and threatened and dominated into submission. And that stays with us, becomes part of our sense of who and what we are. Far better it is to follow our own hearts, make our own decisions, make our own mistakes, and to know, "I am my own person. I can accept myself and respect myself and love myself." Without these inner thoughts and feelings, what are we? We end up with severe limitations.

❦

Besides my father, there arose another possible interference or obstacle for our plan to marry in the spring. Mary Lou had been late for our first date because she had been attending a class for acting and modeling. Like so many newcomers to Southern California—especially those of us who came here as teenagers or young adults—the dream, the fantasy of being discovered and becoming a movie star was floating around in Mary Lou's mind. She took some classes and made a few connections in the field.

When our plans were well under way for our marriage in March, she got a call from an agent about an audition. They were looking for an unknown for the lead in *Two Mules for Sister Sarah*. It could have been a great opportunity. Of course there were no guarantees, but the possibility was there. If she wanted to audition and got the part,

I was ready to either postpone our wedding or get married as planned and postpone our honeymoon.

And she might have gotten the part—Mary Lou was beautiful and sweet, and there was wholesomeness, a freshness about her that might have been perfect for "Sarah". Who knows where that road would have taken her or taken us, but she was hardly tempted by it. I asked her if she wanted to go for it. She told me that she didn't, that she wanted to keep to our plans and be married in the spring. And we did. *Yes, we did, my darling. Thank you again and again and again for keeping to our plans, and for making me and our children and our life together your career.*

Perhaps she would have made it in show business. She had more than enough personality and warmth. Perhaps she would have even beaten the odds and become a star, but would her life have been any better, any fuller, any happier? I don't know. I think probably not.

But then—did I hold her back? I gave her the world—all the travels and restaurants and concerts and shows and anything she wanted that I could give her. And didn't I nourish her soul as she nourished mine? Could I have done more for her? Should I have told her more what I was aware of for so long, that she was a truly remarkable, kind, generous, wonderful, beautiful, lovable angel on earth, that she transformed my life, that she made me so happy for so many years?

Was I a good enough audience of one to witness who she was, or would she have felt better or happier if there had been an audience of millions watching her on the screen?

I wish I had done more to make her aware of how wonderful she was. I should have brought her roses every day of her life. I told her often that I loved her—I should have told her every morning and every evening so that the awareness of her beauty—her inner beauty—would have seeped into her soul, so she would have known that about herself, known at the deepest level of her being.

You did that for me, darling. I wish I had done it more for you. I knew at the time and I told you, but I could have told you more, that I was blessed—truly blessed—to be married to you for thirty-three years.

It should have been like the tefillin, the written commandments that Orthodox Jews bind upon their foreheads and their arms every morning and every evening, so they never lose sight of the truth. I wish I had done that for her, let her know every morning and every evening in every way I could imagine, so she would always have known in her heart, every moment of her life, how remarkable, how wonderful, how full of love and beauty she was.

❧

Mary Lou as a Girl

Mary Lou found her haven behind the barn. With a book and a freshly picked apple, she could escape to another world. No dishes to wash, no food to cook, no laundry to hang—just Mary Lou alone with Zane Gray and *The Riders of the Purple Sage*. She loved those moments. She was sure her mother knew where she was and could have called her to help at any moment, but Erma knew that her daughter needed time for herself. There must be more to life than cleaning and washing and cooking and looking after nine little brothers and sisters. She read to Mary Lou when she was younger—Zane Gray and Mark Twain, the Bible and history of Greece—and filled her head and heart with the desire for adventure, to go beyond her ken, to see the world, to try new things.

As she grew older, Mary Lou reread the books her mother had shared with her and everything else she could find—the histories of Egypt and Europe, the stories of Arabian nights and Robin Hood. She traveled with Jack London to Alaska and solved mysteries with Nancy Drew. Reading became a lifelong habit. She always had a book with her. She read everything but had a special love for mysteries.

Once a friend gave her the book, *The Explorers.* She read about Columbus and Hudson and Magellan, but was particularly fascinated with Henry the Navigator of Portugal. After we were married, we had to go to Portugal to see where he lived and where he set sail to explore the New World, claiming half of it for his country. When she fastened on to a topic or idea, she wouldn't let it go until she had learned everything that she could about it.

Her reading place behind the barn was her sanctuary, but she couldn't always hide. There was work to do, and sooner or later, her mother would call her to help, or one of her brothers or sisters would run up, calling her to play or to help find a lost bunny. She would put her book down and push the dreams of Italy and France and Greece to the back of her mind. She did the work she had to do, and not in anger, without resentment. She knew there was time for herself and there was time when others needed her.

Both of Mary Lou's parents had come from broken homes. Jesse's mother left the family when he was fifteen, and his father left soon after. That meant that he, Jesse, had to take care of himself and his little brother John and two other children, and run the family farm. It was quite a burden for the teenager, but he did it.

Erma's mother abandoned her when she was a little girl, and she was raised by Aunt Lena. She never knew what it was like to have a true mother.

Erma and Jesse were determined and committed to having a family and devoting themselves to loving and caring for their children. They also had an adventurous spirit. They married in Michigan and for their honeymoon went by motorcycle to Niagara Falls and back. Mary Lou, as the only child for three years, basked in their admiration and love. As an infant, she knew or sensed the unconditional, unquestioning, unremitting love that fills the heart and overflows into the world and those around.

Then the other children arrived—Tom and Bev

and Gary and Lodie and Joy and Stan. Soon there wasn't enough time and enough love to go around. Mary Lou's father worked at the Gibson refrigerator plant, but the income wasn't enough to take care of the large family. He worked the swing shift and they bought a small farm. They grew the fruits and vegetables they needed, and raised cows for milk and meat. Jesse worked eight hours in a factory and then many more on the farm.

When Mary Lou was six, her baby brother Gary had whooping cough. The doctor told the parents to be ready for him to die. They prayed, asking God to spare his life, and promised to devote their lives to His work in return. Gary survived and the family became very religious. They joined the Baptist Church and were good to their word— fire-and-brimstone sermons every Sunday, prayer meetings every Wednesday, and tithing of their meagre income. The children sang gospel songs on the radio as the Reinhardt Family Singers, and Mary Lou took her brothers and sisters door-to-door in the neighborhood to evangelize.

Along with the religion came the rules—no movies, no dancing, no smoking, no drinking. But

Erma was too loving to be that strict, and she looked the other way when Mary Lou took one or more of her brothers and sisters to see such movies as *Carousel* or *South Pacific*.

Mary Lou went to a one-room country schoolhouse for her elementary school years. As she grew older, her brothers and sisters joined her in the classroom. Just like home, as one of the oldest, she was asked by the teacher to help look after and teach the younger ones.

Junior and Senior high schools were in Ionia, eight miles from the farm. She was active in a number of clubs, including the science and adventure clubs, and was a cheerleader in her last two years.

Before leaving for nurses' training at Chicago-Swedish Covenant Hospital, her only other time away from home was for a few weeks at a Baptist summer camp, which she didn't like. She felt there were too many rules, and it was too rigid.

But she loved being in Chicago. One of her fondest memories was when she had her own bed in her own room, and on a Saturday night was able to lie in bed smoking a cigarette and drinking a beer. (She later gave up smoking, as we all did.) She attended nurses' training on a partial scholarship. Although it was a hardship, her parents helped with the cost.

Erma and Jesse—especially Erma—embraced Jesus as their savior. The family's life was greatly influenced by the Baptist policies and rituals. Much of Mary Lou's loving nature probably came from the teachings of Jesus and the great example of her mother.

But there were problems with the belief that all good things come from God. Mary Lou was twenty years old when she graduated from nursing school with her degree as a registered nurse. One of the first things she bought with her income was a new dishwasher for her mother. It had not been easy doing the dishes for a family of ten children all those years. Mary Lou arranged for it to be delivered and installed by her brother while their mother was out of the house. When Erma returned, Mary Lou was excited, anticipating her mother's pleasure and surprise and appreciation. And she was surprised and very pleased, but her first words were to praise Jesus. Mary Lou was devastated. She choked back the words that were forming in her throat about her part in this "miracle", and where the credit belonged.

No, Mary Lou didn't get any credit—She was simply an instrument of God. It was a problem for all of her life. No matter how many people praised her—for her talent as an artist, for kindness, for her unfailing acknowledgement of other people's happy events, for her beauty, for the goodness of her soul—it was as if she couldn't take the praise in and own it as part of herself, part of her being. She turned away from praise, and she suffered for it. She wasn't able to know how truly remarkable, how truly love-filled, how truly beautiful she was inside and out.

Soon after she started earning money as a nurse, Mary Lou began to buy things for everyone in her family. She made a point of taking each one of her brothers and sisters—alone, just the two of them—for an adventure. Often it was to drive the three miles from the farm to the Dairy Queen in Saranac, population two thousand. Each child enjoyed the milkshake or ice cream treat with big sister Mary

Lou, knowing and feeling that he or she was special and loved.

She also saved some of her earnings and used much of it for needed items on the farm, including a new refrigerator.

Most of the clothes that the children wore were hand-me-downs, from the church or a second-hand store. Once the items were in the family, they went from one child to the next younger and then on and on. When Mary Lou was twenty-two, she drove home from work one weekend with a present for her eighteen-year-old sister. Bev looked at the box, shook it, and tried to guess the contents, but Mary Lou wouldn't give away the secret. Finally Bev opened the box, and there, nestled in the crisp tissue, was the first new dress that she had ever owned.

❧

The population of Saranac was two thousand at that time. The highlight of a Saturday night was to go to the Dairy Queen for a milkshake. The mayor asked Mary Lou to represent the town in the Ionia County beauty pageant. She won and became Miss Saranac and Miss Ionia County. She entered the Miss Michigan Pageant, part of the Miss America pageant, and was one of the finalists for the state.

As with many beautiful girls in the world, the dream of Hollywood was in her head. After graduating with her nursing degree, she returned to live on the farm and work in the local hospital, but her energy and sense of adventure were so great that she had to leave. When she was twenty-three, she put her belongings into her seven-year-old two-door Chevrolet "Murphy" (Mary Lou liked to name things) and set out for Los Angeles.

❧

She moved into a small apartment near Sunset Strip in Hollywood, the area of Sunset Boulevard known for its restaurants, clubs and cafes. One of her patients during this time was Si Zentner, the big band leader. She took care of him in the hospital for several months and became friends with him and his wife and their daughter, who was Mary Lou's age.

After he recovered and his band was getting ready to go on tour again, Linda, his daughter, asked Mary Lou if she would like to travel in the bus with the band all over the country. A chance for travel? Adventure? Of course! Mary Lou was packed and ready.

They traveled for several months as the band performed in Chicago, Des Moines, and many smaller cities. One of the band's favorite numbers was *The Stripper*. During one of the performances, Mary Lou was sitting at a table, and Linda handed her one of her long over-the-elbow black gloves. Mary Lou started to play with it in rhythm to the music. Si saw what she was doing and motioned for her to come up before the band. As they continued to play, Mary Lou did her strip—moving the gloves slowly and rhythmically over her shoulders, hands and behind her body. The audience loved it. Si asked her to do it whenever the band played that number, and it became part of their routine.

There were times in later years that Mary Lou did a much better private strip for me. And as beautiful and desirable as she was, her Baptist background and her wholesomeness was always there. She was more adorable than sexy, too cute to be a real vamp.

The tour ended and Mary Lou returned to her apartment and to special-duty nursing. We met soon after that.

Marriage

We were married in a traditional reformed Jewish ceremony on March 26,1967. We vowed to love, honor and cherish each other, but Mary Lou did more than that, and I tried to do more for her too. If I were writing our vows today I would promise the following:

I will love you.
I will honor you.
I will cherish you.
I will do everything in my power to nourish
*   your soul and to enrich your life.*

That is what she did for me and what I tried to do for her. We promised to love, honor and cherish each other until death do us part. Now I am not sure about "until death do us part". Perhaps the reality is that love exists until we both are dead. I know in my head that people heal from a loss like this. The knowledge hasn't reached my heart yet.

Two hearts o'er time
Grown as one.
One is taken—
Does love from love arise?
Or does the other shrivel
To join again the one that's taken?

Most of my family was at our wedding—my mother and father, my brother and sister-in-law, my niece and nephew, both my Aunt Katherine and Aunt Dorothy, and my cousins. Only Mary Lou's sister Bev attended from her side. The others simply couldn't afford to come, but I felt they accepted and loved me and were pleased that we married.

Honeymoon
Japan

We started our honeymoon with the flight from Los Angeles to Tokyo, and it felt like it took three weeks. I had jet lag for three days after we arrived, but once we had adjusted to the time change, we were off and running.

Mary Lou wanted to see everything, go everyplace, and do everything. We walked the stairs up to the top of the Tokyo Tower and our legs were sore for days afterward. We saw the Deer Park in Nara.

Our most memorable experience in Japan was a four-night stay in Kyoto in a ryokan—a small inn. Kyoto is the beautiful spiritual and cultural center of Japan. Our room was tiny and simple. We slept on futons on the floor made of tatami mats. We had our dinners at the hotel's three-seat Sushi bar. We walked the streets and went to the temples. We smiled and tried to talk to the children.

One night as we were finishing at the sushi bar, the chef asked us if we would like a massage in our room. We agreed to it, and a half-hour later, two very elderly Japanese ladies knocked on our door. They bowed, and we bowed. They bowed again. We motioned for them to enter. They motioned for us to remove our clothes and lie down on the mats. Each of the ladies looked as though she weighed no more than ninety pounds, but their hands had the strength of sumo wrestlers. They rubbed and kneaded our bodies as we lay side by side on the mats. Occasionally, they would look at Mary Lou and start to giggle, first about her gold earrings and then it was her painted fingernails. They were having a good time, and we were too. We didn't realize at the time that the giggling masseurs and a three-seat sushi bar would be printed indelibly into our memories—a memory that would last the rest of our lives.

Hong Kong

In the Orient for the first month of our trip, we stayed at very good hotels. We were unfamiliar with the cities and cultures and felt we needed that extra security.

In Hong Kong, we stayed at the Hilton. One afternoon when we returned to the hotel, we looked around the lobby and thought there had been a disaster. People were strewn all over. Every seat, every sofa was taken. The people in them were stretched out with a dazed look, as though they had been in a war or hadn't slept in a week. I sat down next to one of the couples and asked them what had happened. They said that they had checked in but their rooms weren't ready yet. When I asked why everyone looked as if they had been in a riot or hadn't slept, I was told that they all worked for Westinghouse and were winners of an in-house contest for the most productive, most sales, most increases in revenue. Their prize was an eighteen-day around-the-world trip. They hadn't been in the same hotel for more than two nights and couldn't even remember what the last city was. They didn't know if it was 4:00 p.m. or 4:00 a.m. or if the next meal should be dinner or breakfast. It wasn't a prize—It was a punishment!

Mary Lou and I learned a valuable lesson from that. We were never in a hurry. If we liked where we were, we stayed. When we were ready to move on, we went to the next city. We never stayed less than three nights in one hotel or inn, and we often stayed a week or even longer.

We had clothes made in Hong Kong. (Years later, after having given birth to three children, Mary Lou could still fit into the suit and the skirts and blouses that she had made there.) We had dinner on a floating restaurant, and as we enjoyed the Peking duck, a grandfather played the lute for us while his granddaughter sang.

We went to the top of Victoria Peak at ten o'clock at night. I tried to take a time exposure of the beautiful harbor and ships below us. I didn't know the necessary time setting, though, so none of the pictures came out. The evening stayed with us anyway.

Remember, Darling—standing of the deck of a Chinese junk, the Hong Kong harbor.

We went on the evening harbor dinner cruise, and I took the picture of Mary Lou that is in on the cover of this book. There were two American pilots on the cruise. We started talking with them. They were on rest and rehabilitation from their service, and told us what it was like to fly fighter jets—the thrill, the excitement, the exhilaration of risking their lives.

One of them told us about his girlfriend back home and the other told us about his fiancée. As they talked of how much they missed their girls—how much they wanted to just hold hands and walk with them and talk—they were looking at Mary

Lou. For each of those men, she became the girl back home—the same beauty, the same friendliness. They just wanted to be with us—really just with Mary Lou—as close as they could be, halfway around the world, to the ones they loved. Mary Lou had a natural grace, an innate ability to make people feel comfortable and accepted and loved.

I took a picture of her then, *"...your hair blowing in the gentle breeze. Your eyes sparkling against the just before twilight darkening blue sky. My twenty-five-year-old bride—Your beautiful face, filled with love, filled with happiness, filled with the promise of our future together."*

Did I know? How could I know the depths of her love, the beauty of her person, the gifts that she brought to me, to our marriage and to our life together? Her greatest treasures were veiled behind her physical beauty. More precious than rubies, than diamonds, than sapphires or gold...

All the riches in the world are nothing compared to the precious gifts of a true and loving heart. There is nothing on this earth that can compare with the treasures from her heart that she gave so freely to me.

I wish I had told her
every day
in every way
in the morning
and in the evening —

I love you, I cherish you
beyond words, beyond rubies,
You are my treasure —

Until it seeped into her being,
seeped into her soul,
and she knew
She was loved,
Loved beyond words,
Loved beyond all else,
Loved beyond all measure.

Thailand—Bangkok

In Bangkok, we stayed at the InterContinental Hotel, a beautiful hotel in the style of a temple, with high domes the color of brilliant orange saffron. On a tour of the clongs (canals) of Bangkok, our narrow boat took us through the waterways filled with other boats carrying chickens and vegetables and fruits. This was the city's market. We went past homes perched on tiny slender stilts that held them above the water. We saw the children swimming in the water and women washing their clothes—all of the city's life existing on and in the water.

Our dinner one night at the hotel was accompanied by a performance of the beautiful Thai dancers with painted faces, moving through their steps in the traditionally slow and deliberate way. After dinner, we sat by the pool as the sun set. It was so lovely and tranquil, and suddenly so infested with mosquitoes. They were all over us, and we were swatting as fast as our hands could move, but they were biting us even faster. That night, and for the next few nights, our bodies were covered with welts from the bites.

We went to a Thai kickboxing fight in an old boxing arena, and sat on dirty seats on old dilapidated benches with the rest of the crowd of screaming and jumping Thais. The combination of boxing and kicking was very exciting. After the last match of the evening as we were filing out along with everyone else, the plank that Mary Lou stepped on gave way, and her foot plunged through the opening in the floor. I grabbed her to prevent her from falling any further. A piece of dirty jagged wood like a stalagmite was jutting out toward her and stopped just inches away from her pelvis. We were so fortunate—She could have been so badly injured if not killed.

Greece—Athens

When we got to Athens, we decided that we had to send most of our clothes home. We went to the American Express office, and shipped all we could allow ourselves to part with. We were down to one medium-sized suitcase for the two of us, and we had four more months of travel. I had two pairs of pants, underwear, three shirts, socks and two pairs of shoes. Mary Lou was traveling equally light. She was down to two dresses. One of them was a flowered print dress, and she wore it everywhere.

When we finally got back to Los Angeles, I asked her politely and tactfully to burn that dress. Twenty-five years later, she came into the family room modeling what I thought was a new purchase. When she asked how I liked her new dress, I didn't recognize it. After twenty-five years and three children, she was still able to wear it, and she still looked great in it.

—Santorini

Mary Lou had a hard time throwing anything away. Growing up in poverty had a lot to do with it, but she also felt that everything had a memory attached to it. When we went to Greece for the first time, we fell in love with the country, and especially Santorini

The ferry let us off by the dock and we went by mule to the top of the island. The view of the Aegean Sea was magnificent. We had a wonderful salad lunch with feta cheese and wine. The narrow cobblestone streets at the top of Santorini are lined with small shops, and Mary Lou bought a pair of sandals in one. She loved those sandals. On our many trips back to Greece, we had to go to the same shop and she would buy four or six more pairs, enough to last her until the next visit. She wore the same sandals almost everywhere— to the movies, to dinner, to shows, in summer and winter.

It wasn't about style or cost or even comfort. It was about memories and happiness and love.

—Mykonos

The cheapest way to get from Athens to Mykonos is to take the nine-hour ferry that leaves from Piraeus. I get seasick very easily but on this trip, the sea was calm, and we both felt good but tired when we arrived just past midnight. We had no reservations but some of the villagers of Mykonos who have rooms to rent meet the ferry. As we walked off the ship, a friendly looking old woman approached us and asked if we would like a very nice clean inexpensive room. We replied that we would and followed her through the narrow dark street to her home. The price was $1.65 per night, breakfast included. The room was tiny, as were the two hard twin beds. We were so tired that we slept until the brilliant sunlight streaming through the windows awoke us the next morning.

We washed and went out to ask the woman about breakfast. She ushered us into a little garden with a white marble table in the middle. The area was covered by an arbor of green leaves and brown grapevines. On top of a nearby marble pillar, a big black cat was dozing in the morning sun. Bright red geraniums hung down from the vines. We sat at the table and our hostess brought us coffee, freshly baked bread, and honeyed yogurt. We stayed at her home for a week. The beds were terrible, but the breakfasts in that sunlit garden were among the most delicious meals we ever had.

We explored Mykonos, walking through the tiny streets, and sat at the seaside cafe in the afternoon and had glasses of wine. Peter the Pelican was the regular guest of honor, more like a mayor than a guest. He wandered from table to table snatching bits of bread and meat from friendly hands.

One day as we were sitting at the café, we noticed a young man going from table to table talking to everyone. At one table, he would speak English, and at the next, it was French, then German. We wondered what it was all about until he finally came to our table. In that wonderful brogue of the Irish, he told us of a beach party that would be happening on the other side of the bay that night. He asked if we would like to attend, and we asked about the transportation, if the food would be good, what the cost would be. His answers satisfied us and we paid him. He told us to meet him at seven o'clock and to come hungry and thirsty.

There must have been sixty or seventy of us there. Patrick, the party-giver, put us into small boats that he had hired. The local fishermen took us across the bay to the far shore, and as we got off the boat, Patrick told us where to sit. Out came barrels of wine and some bread, and then retsina, a dreadful drink I've never been able to develop a taste for. Whenever we go to another country, I try to eat the foods of that country and drink the wine or liquor while I'm there. I have no problem with ouzo or cognac or champagne or slivovitz. But I have a problem with retsina, and just can't seem to enjoy it. Fortunately, Patrick also had several barrels of regular wine. We sat on the beach, drank the wine and passed the bread around. Two pigs were roasted on a spit. When they were done, each of us received some of the meat along with whatever we needed to eat it. I was amazed at how well he had planned and carried out everything.

The best part was yet to come. After we all had enough to eat and drink, sitting on the beach with wood fires burning to keep us warm, Patrick asked if anyone had a story to tell.

An Irish friend of his told the first story. Then Patrick told one, and then a German girl. A French boy told his, and then there was another from Patrick. If you've ever heard an Irishman tell a story in his brogue, then you know that there is something magical about Irish storytellers. We sat through the night absolutely enthralled. We listened to story after story, joke after a joke, told by Americans, Irishmen, French, Germans, Dutch. The fires never went out, and we stayed there until dawn. Then the fisherman returned with their boats and ferried us all back to Mykonos.

Patrick, wherever you are—Thank you for that night. I hope the wind has always been at your back and the sun has always shone on your face. And I hope you have traveled a happy and fulfilled road.

Austria —Vienna

Remember, darling—our first opera together.

We arrived at the Vienna airport late in the afternoon. Trusting in our well-worn copy of *Europe on $5 a Day*, we found a cab and asked the driver to take us to the Graben Hotel. The hotel was on a very narrow street, and the cabby had to let us off at St. Stephensplatz, about a hundred yards from the hotel. We carried our suitcase into the alley and entered the tiny lobby of the hotel. We had no reservation but we did have luck, and the desk clerk had a room for us,

Before showing the room, he started to tell us about the opera that night. It was hard enough to understand what he was saying because of his accent and we didn't understand German. But after he spoke a few words, we realized that he was drunk. He was trying to tell us about the opera, show us the room, and carry our suitcase up the narrow stairway all at the same time. He was too drunk to do one, let alone all three at the same time. We told him that we were tired, that we had been traveling all day. All we wanted to do was go to the room, take a bath (which was down the hall), get a bite to eat, and go to sleep.

He was persistent about the opera, though, and told us he could get marvelous seats for us. He was most emphatic. It almost seemed as though he wasn't going to let us have the room unless we agreed to go to the opera. We agreed to go. His face, already flushed from drinking, seemed to turn an even brighter shade of red, but this time from pleasure instead of from alcohol. He tried to carry our remaining suitcase up the stairs but was too drunk to make it, so we took it ourselves, found the room, walked down the hallway to the bath and then back to our room.

When Mary Lou slipped under the eiderdown quilt and crawled under the sheets for a moment's rest, she told me how heavenly it was, that she didn't want to leave. But the desk clerk had finally made it up the stairs and was knocking on our door, telling us we had to go right then. The opera was to start in twenty minutes and if we hurried, we could walk there. All of this was spoken in drunken slurred German that we could barely understand.

We reluctantly got out of that cozy warm bed, dressed, and following the clerk's directions, walked to the Vienna Opera House clutching our tickets in our hands.

The "marvelous seats" turned out to be standing room only, but the Vienna Opera House is small by most standards and seats less than two thousand people. Standing room is at the back on the orchestra level where there is a wall about four feet high. We had an excellent view of the stage, and the music was wonderfully close. There were two folding chairs in the back, and whenever anyone got tired, he or she could sit down for a few moments. There was a great sense of friendship and cooperation among those of us who shared the area.

I had attended several operas before. When I was a teen-ager, the parents of my good friend Bernie had taken us to the Metropolitan Opera in New York a few times, but I didn't get hooked back then. This was Mary Lou's first time.

The opera began—It was *Madame Butterfly*. The music seemed to flow around us and into us and through us, holding us in its romantic love-filled arms. As the story unfolded, we were drawn into her world—her love, her warmth, her sacrifice. I could hardly take my eyes off the stage. It was unbelievably beautifully done. At the same time, I didn't want to stop looking at Mary Lou. She was enraptured, captured, absolutely totally thrilled. She was glued to every moment and every sound coming from the stage. When I asked if she wanted to sit down for a moment, she shushed me, telling me to be quiet so she could listen.

During the entr'acte between the third and fourth acts, Madame Butterfly waits out the night, waits for love and Pinkerton to return to her after years of absence. The music is filled with longing and love and sadness. Mary Lou and I have seen the opera several times since that first, but we have never seen it done as beautifully as that night. Madame Butterfly was in a kimono, standing against the pale blue windows that showed the changing night sky beyond. Her arms were raised so that the folds of her kimono hung down like wings of a fragile butterfly. She looked as though she were pinned against the night sky. I have never experienced a more beautiful and moving moment of opera than that scene with its glorious music and image.

And Mary Lou was there, in standing room only, after a day's travel, without supper, for the three hours of the opera—transfixed. I saw her tears. I saw her smile. I saw her heart and her soul open to the world of Puccini. I saw her blossoming before my eyes.

I don't think she knew before that night who Puccini was, or had heard much or any of this music. Her exposure had been to the gospel hymns at church and some of the Broadway musicals that had been made into movies—*Carousel* and *South Pacific* and *Sound of Music*— and she loved the contemporary hit songs of Buddy Holly and the Big Bopper.

That night of *Madame Butterfly*, the music and the story went straight to her heart, and resonated with her being. She was hooked—We were both hooked. For this, I am eternally grateful to that drunken desk clerk at the Graben Hotel just off St. Stephensplatz in Vienna. Little did he know when he saw two newlyweds enter his hotel— tired, obviously in love, unsophisticated, hungry— that he was going to coerce us into a life-changing, life-enriching experience.

For the rest of our honeymoon, we went to opera every time we had a chance. The next night, we went back to the Vienna Opera and saw Mozart's *Cosi fan Tutte*. Two nights later, we went to the Theater An der Wein, People's Opera, and saw *The Merry Widow*, all in German. The language didn't matter—It was the music and the images and the glorious voices. With the help of the desk clerk, we could get tickets for everything. He wasn't as drunk the next time that we saw him.

Perhaps he was beaming that way because he saw what a marvelous effect he had on us.

Mary Lou was always ready to show our appreciation, and whenever we went walking to the museums and shops of Vienna, if we bought pastries, she always brought back a piece of strudel or torte just in case our clerk was there.

In *Europe on $5 a Day*, Arthur Frommer described a youth cafeteria where a hearty breakfast was only fifty cents. The cafeteria was three blocks from the hotel, and one morning we decided to try it. There was a problem in Vienna, though— You couldn't walk three blocks in any direction without passing at least two pastry shops. We had gone less than one block when we looked into a window and saw a tempting chocolate puff of sweetness. We decided to share one before we had our breakfast. In the next block, we saw a lemon eclair in another window, and decided to try it as well. We never made it to the cafeteria, but we did stop at eight pastry shops within two hours. We rated that experience as comparable to our two hours at the Kunsthistoriche Museum looking at the Brueghels and the Vermeers.

Italy—Milan

Before we reached Italy, we had arranged to buy a car in Milan. We arrived by plane, and by the time we picked up the car, it was early evening, and we didn't have any hotel reservations. There we were, in this new fire engine red Fiat 850 two-passenger convertible, driving through Milan, trying to find a tiny hotel in a city we didn't know.

We got caught in a traffic loop and seemed to be going around and 'round in a four or five mile circle in the center of the city. Mary Lou was frantically trying to read the street signs and I was equally frantic trying to get out of that loop. We stopped at a red light, with a car to the left and a car to the right with a small space between us. I looked into the rearview mirror and saw a car barreling down on us. I could see that it was headed for the space to our right, but I also saw that there wasn't enough room. Bam! The driver tried for the space and slammed on his brakes as his car bumped into our right front fender.

Our new car! Less than ten miles on it! I was enraged. I jumped out, pulled the driver's door of the other car open, and started hollering at the driver. Mary Lou must have gone into shock. She soon recovered and tried to calm me down. As I did, I noticed that there were four very big, strong-looking Italian men in the other car.

There didn't seem to be anything to do. The other driver was talking in Italian and I think he was apologizing, but who knows? We were tying up traffic on this main thoroughfare through the city. There were no policemen, so we just drove off, waving goodbye to the other driver and the other occupants. In retrospect, I was grateful that he and his burly friends were not as mad as I was. Perhaps they viewed my outrage as part of everyday life. It could have become very ugly.

Mary Lou had never seen me that angry before, and I could remember only a few times in my life when I've been like that. She was quiet for a long time before telling me how much I had frightened her. She said she hadn't seen me like that before and it reminded her of her father when he got furious at her brothers, sometimes beating them with a strap.

❧

She told me about her father's anger. Erma and Jesse were among the hardest working people I've ever known. There was cooking and washing and cleaning and hanging out the laundry and gardening and dishes and diapers and feeding of the children. Jesse worked eight hours in a factory and longer hours on the farm.

I think his anger started to get the better of him after the family took in the three small children who had been left on the doorstep of the church. An impoverished mother had abandoned them, leaving a note. "Please, God, take care of my babies. I can't do it." The minister's sermon praying for a loving family to take these poor children went straight to Erma's heart. Jesse didn't want to but he felt it was God's will.

Suzy and Lyle and Lee, all under four years of age, became part of the family. It meant more work for Erma and Jesse and more pressure on the older girls, Mary Lou and Bev. Jesse would lose his temper at times, when one of the boys didn't do what he had been told. He would take the boy to the cellar, take off his belt, and beat him until he'd exhausted his anger.

When Mary Lou was fourteen, she told her mother that if she had any more babies, she would run away. Erma and Jesse didn't intend to have any more but they didn't do much to prevent it either.

When Stanley came along, Mary Lou didn't leave home. She was like a mother to this little brother. She buried her anger and resentment and gave out love. She bathed Stanley, and fed him, and changed his diapers. She always said that babies had a special place in her heart. Stanley was more like her own baby than like a brother.

But what was the cost to her? She always had difficulty feeling anger, and an even harder time expressing it towards anyone. She was quick to forgive, and quick to give her love. Those are wonderful traits, but they prevented her from being assertive. She had difficulty advancing her needs, or asking for what she wanted and needed for herself. Living at home, there was always the fear of Jesse's rage, and so she kept her wishes to herself.

Perhaps Mary Lou saw that same streak of anger and rage in me. So often we seek a partner or lover who is like one of our parents, hoping to finally get what is needed from him or her. Maybe the long years of my psychoanalysis helped resolve some of my anger, but by far the greatest factor was Mary Lou's love.

My love, your love has healed me, subdued the anger, released the resentment.

❧

—Naples

We did our homework before we arrived in different cities. We read (or rather Mary Lou read, since she was the researcher) about the beautiful port area of Naples, and that it was the birthplace of pizza, which we had to try. We had also read about the Opera House, the Teatro di San Carlo. The day we arrived, we learned that there was to be a performance of *Lucia di Lammermoor* that night. We didn't need to be coerced this time, and bought our tickets.

It is a small intimate opera house, the smallest I've ever been in, seating less than a thousand people. Our seats were in the first balcony on the side. At the end of the third act, Lucia sings her mad aria scene accompanied by a single flute. At the end of the ten minutes of this incredibly gorgeous aria, she stabs herself and falls dead on the stage as the curtain closes.

I have never seen an audience react as they did that night—All one thousand people stood and shouted, "Bravo! Bravo! Bravo!" All of this was accompanied by stamping of feet and throwing flowers onto the stage. The ovation went on and on and on for twenty minutes. Mary Lou and I shouted as loudly as everyone else did. That night, I felt we were Italians. "Bravo! Bravo! Bravo!" The soprano was so pleased that she repeated the entire aria. The second ovation and bravos and flowers went on for another ten minutes.

Sometimes, in the midst of an experience, you don't know until later the importance, the impact, the influence and intense pleasure that will remain. That was the case with the memory of the strudel and pastry. But in other moments as they happen, it is clear that they are indelible and will stay with you forever. For us, that was *Butterfly* in Vienna, and *Lucia* in Naples, and *Carmen* in Paris. For me, that was being married to Mary Lou.

—Assisi

The lodging we found in Assisi from *Europe on $5 a Day* was drab. The twin beds looked seedy, but we arrived late in the day and didn't want to look any further. We put our suitcase in the room, took baths, and in the evening, went out to eat.

We found an inexpensive restaurant nearby. As we were enjoying a really good bottle of inexpensive wine with dinner, a group of very happy young men came in and sat at tables near us. They were boisterous—singing and hugging each other. We asked them what they were celebrating. They told us that they had just won the soccer championship of Assisi. Mary Lou suggested to me that we send over a bottle of wine, and we told the waiter our wishes. He delivered a bottle to them, and they raised their glasses to us and said, "Grazzi— Saluté!"

The waiter then brought another bottle to our table. We had just about finished our bottle and told him we hadn't ordered another, but he said it was from the soccer team. We couldn't offend them, so we filled and raised our glasses to them. "Saluté!"

We finished both bottles of wine. It was a good thing that our hotel was only a few steps away because we couldn't have gone very far. We plopped into our bed and slept until late the next day. We slept so soundly that we didn't notice that bed bugs were feasting on us. Those bites itched and we scratched for days until the swelling went down. It was worth it, though—the unforgettable night we celebrated with the championship soccer team of Assisi.

—Venice

When we arrived in Venice, we went straight to

St. Mark's Square. We had our large suitcase with us and needed to find a hotel, but Mary Lou was captivated by the pigeons. She bought a small bag of rice and held some out in her hand. Soon she was surrounded by the birds. We sat at one of the cafes bordering the square and ordered glasses of wine. It was idyllic.

Our five dollars of expense money for that day was spent in its entirety when I asked the leader of the four-piece musical group if they would play something by Vivaldi. They played *Spring* from *The Four Seasons*. We had sunshine and wine, birds eating out of Mary Lou's hand, and four musicians playing one of our favorite pieces. It was springtime in Venice and springtime in our hearts. It was springtime in our lives and the world was beautiful.

We still needed to find a hotel, though, and our search took us to a small one just off the square. It was quite a bargain for the fair-sized room, and we could even see the square from the window looking out the third floor.

It wasn't until the next morning that we discovered why the price was so cheap. At six every morning, the clock tower came to life. Two bronze angels emerged and marched from each side of the tower. As they came around to the front, they slammed their hammers into the bell. I think it even woke people in Florence as well as everyone in Venice.

We were able to fall back to sleep, but this was an hourly event from 6:00 a.m. until 8:00 p.m. We stayed in that hotel for five nights. Who needs to sleep when you're young and in love and on your honeymoon? By the second morning, we realized that we had the best room in all of Venice. The six a.m. clock tower show was a reminder that it was time to wake up and make love again.

Oh my darling, remember how our hearts sang and our bodies danced?

From each place we visited, Mary Lou wanted to bring back a souvenir. We brought back trinkets from everywhere—little inexpensive toy flowers or glasses, dolphins or a scarf— anything as long it was as it was part of where we were. Soon we could barely carry our luggage.

As we were leaving Venice, walking through St. Mark's Square to the vaparetto (the little motor boat that would take us through the canals to where our car was parked), I had our big suitcase on my shoulder. It was now too heavy to carry any other way. Mary Lou wanted to take my picture, but the light wasn't just right. She asked me to walk in a circle until the angle was good, and then to circle around her again, and then again, and then again. I finally blew up and told her to take the damn picture, that the suitcase was killing me.

Austria—Salzburg

Salzburg means music and Mozart to me. I don't remember where we stayed or any of the restaurants we went to for dinner, but I do remember most vividly walking on a cobblestone street looking for Mozart's birthplace. As we were walking, we heard music—two flutes— coming from somewhere. We walked in that direction and soon came to an archway covered with the same cobblestones as the street. In the most distant part of the arch surrounded by stone were two young people, probably teenagers. They were leaning against the wall, a hat for tips in front of them, and playing flutes. I didn't recognize what they were playing but it sounded like and probably was something by Mozart.

The acoustics of their location were unbelievable. The music bounced and resonated and echoed all around us. I can't imagine a better place or a better sound. We stood and listened with a dozen other people, and then we all applauded and put some shillings into their hat. What a gift those two young people gave to us and to everyone else who was there! Not only did Mary Lou and I enjoy a serendipitous concert, we also learned a lesson, a lesson that we lived by—*follow the music!*

Germany—Munich

One evening in Munich, we stood with dozens of other tourists and a few townspeople in front of the cathedral with our heads thrown back to see the clock high up on the tower. As the clock reached the hour, we watched and listened as the stone and metal burghers marched from behind the bell around to the front and diligently struck the hour. Then they obediently marched back and took their places to wait for the next hour.

We then went to the Rathskellar, a large restaurant in the cellar of the town hall. It had a boisterous and friendly atmosphere, with people enjoying the hearty food, the wine and beer, and talking from table to table.

We were midway through our dinner when three Frenchman at the next table finished theirs. As they were leaving, they stopped and asked us in French how we liked the restaurant. I had studied French for three years in high school and four in college and had lived in France for two years while I was in the Air Force. I thought that I could speak the language reasonably well and confidently responded in French that we were enjoying it greatly, that we liked the food and the friendly atmosphere. They nodded briefly at me as they continued to gaze at Mary Lou. They then said, "Bon nuit" (good night). Mary Lou answered, "Bon nuit." The Frenchmen exploded with compliments— "Magnifique! What a wonderful accent! You speak French so well. You must have grown up in France. Where did you live in France?"

Mary Lou smiled. I think they were hoping we would ask them to join us for dessert, but they had drunk a little too much wine for that. Mary Lou smiled and said, "Adieux" and "Bon nuit". As they were leaving, they kept looking over their shoulders, smiling and waving at her all the way. She kept waving and smiling at them as they left. She smiled many times afterward as she recalled the night she spoke fluent French—and with such a wonderful accent!

France—Vienne

One of our honeymoon splurges was dinner at a three-star restaurant in Vienne, France. The restaurant was elegant, and one of the attractions was the small hotel that was part of the experience—Le Residence des Pyramides.

We drove into town in our little two-seater convertible, and arrived late in the afternoon. We checked into the hotel and then strolled around the village square looking at the shops. We sat at an outdoor cafe and had wine. As we were returning, we saw a couple drive up to the hotel in a new Jaguar. The woman was stunning, with jet black hair swept up into a bun on top of her head, flawless skin, and an elegant silk dress of rich burgundy color. He was straight out of the movies, as handsome as Louis Jourdan. To us, they were the epitome of French class and culture.

As we changed for dinner, Mary Lou put on her best (or shall I say, her better) dress, and I put on my better pair of khakis, shirt with tie and jacket. We walked the three blocks to the restaurant along with other couples who were staying at the hotel.

The dining room was large and rectangular with a gigantic array of flowers in the center. Mary Lou and I had a lovely table close to the flowers. The elegant French couple was a few tables away from us. Mary Lou had her back to them but I could see them clearly over her shoulder. I watched and described what was going on to her.

First they ordered a bottle of white wine with their appetizers. As they were drinking, I could see their hands touch and hold each other under the table. I saw her hand slip under the table and gently stroke his thigh. They ordered a bottle of rosé wine and proceeded to drink that, accompanied by a new round of caressing. He even got up from his chair, walked around to her and kissed her. Next came a bottle of red wine. Mary Lou was dying to see all of this but she would have had to turn very noticeably and rudely to see them, so I continued to describe what I was seeing.

As they were finishing the third bottle of wine, she began to hiccup, and her face turned ashen white. Sweat broke out on her forehead. As her face turned green, she began to make a sucking noise that was followed by an explosive sound. She threw up all over their table—Out came the white wine, the rosé, the red, the appetizers, the entree, the dessert—with a smattering onto the man's jacket and the floor. Suddenly, her head fell to the table, and she lay there in a stupor.

I then saw why the restaurant deserved its three-star honors. Out came a troupe of waiters. Two of them lifted her gently from the table. Others expertly whisked away the dishes and the tablecloth. One waiter appeared with a washcloth to help with the man's jacket. Another appeared with a mop and bucket and cleaned the floor. A fresh tablecloth was spread, clean dishes and silverware laid.

The couple was helped out of the restaurant in less than ten minutes, and the area looked as if the incident had never occurred. Mary Lou and I continued and finished our dinner, and then had a lovely stroll through the park back to the hotel.

The next morning as we were putting our suitcase into our car, we looked up toward the second story of the hotel. Hanging over the railing, drying in the sun, was a beautiful burgundy silk dress.

Spain—Madrid

One evening when we were in Madrid, we started out for dinner, looking for a tiny restaurant recommended in our guidebook. Before long, we were in a dark deserted area, lost and feeling unsafe. We saw no one.

As we were wandering, looking in our book and at our map, a man approached us from the other side of the street. Only the three of us were there. He wore a faded shirt and khakis and looked poor. He spoke to us in Spanish. Living in Southern California, we had heard a lot of Spanish, and Mary Lou worked with many Spanish-speaking nurses and aides at the hospital. She'd never studied it but she had a wonderful ear for languages. She understood that he was asking if we were lost and needed help, and she pointed to the name of the restaurant in the book. He told us to follow him, that he'd take us there.

We walked with him for three or four dark deserted city streets. Soon we came to a street with several small restaurants. He took us into one of them, the one for which we had been searching. He told us that he was a truck driver and was spending the night in Madrid, and that we were in a very inexpensive part of the city.

The front area of the restaurant was a small bar that served tapas—the Spanish hors d'oeuvres. He asked us if we would join him for a glass of wine and insisted on paying. When we asked if we could buy him another glass, he declined and wished us a good evening. He said that we would enjoy the food there, and with an "adios", he left.

We returned to Madrid a number of times, have seen the museums, and stayed at the finest hotels, eaten at the city's best restaurants. None of those experiences, as wonderful as they were, made as great an impression on us as the simple honesty, graciousness and dignity of that Spanish truck driver who went out of his way to be kind and generous to two young Americans lost and fearful in a strange city.

S.S. HOPE

When Mary Lou was in nurses' training in Chicago, a visiting nurse gave a lecture to the class that affected Mary Lou and subsequently me and our life together. The nurse had been on the S.S. HOPE, a hospital ship that was part of Project HOPE, started in 1958 by William B. Walsh. An internist from Washington, D.C. during the Eisenhower presidency, Walsh was a charismatic person, a magnificent speaker and an outstanding fundraiser—a man with a vision.

The U.S. Navy donated one of its hospital ships, the S.S. Repose, to the Project. Funds were raised; the ship was refitted and staff hired. The first voyage took place in 1960. The ship's mission was to travel to underdeveloped countries of the world, treat the sick, and train medical personnel of the host countries in Western-style medicine. Mary Lou listened and was captivated. The lecture stayed with her and became part of her dreams of traveling beyond her ken.

When we returned from our honeymoon, we lived in a suburb of Los Angeles. Once again, I did locum tenens for pediatricians in the area and Mary Lou did special-duty nursing. Her dream of the S.S. Hope re-emerged. We talked about it, weighed the pros and cons, and finally applied to be part the ship's next journey to Ceylon (now Sri Lanka).

We joined the ship in Fort Lauderdale and sailed off with two hundred other "Hopies". During the first week of the six-week voyage, I had such a bad case of cabin fever that I was ready to jump ship and swim the rest of the way. After a week, we all settled into the routine of the ship, a schedule that started with breakfast, a lecture or discussion group about working in an undeveloped country, and reviews of some of the medical conditions we expected to encounter. The highlight of the day was an afternoon bridge tournament that went on week after week. Dinner was in the ship's dining room.

As we headed close to the equator with the warmer

nights, we would set up our table on deck and have dinner there. It was serene. Time was endless. We didn't care how long the voyage took. One day was just like the next and we were all comfortable with the routine and soon comfortable with each other.

Finally we arrived at the port city of Colombo, the capital of Ceylon. We were welcomed with open arms by some, but hadn't realized that there were powerful people who opposed our presence. We were seen by them and written about in the papers as U.S. government spies. They wrote that we were there to prevent the Communists from taking over the country, and to spread disease, not to fight it.

Each Hopie at every level—physician, nurse, aide, technician—had a Ceylonese counterpart. We worked side by side, sometimes on the ship and other times in one of the local hospitals. Friendships developed and trust soon followed.

I was in charge of the pediatric department, and Mary Lou was one of the pediatric nurses. Ceylon is the only place in the world where Singalese is the native language. Mary Lou had a natural ear and talent for languages, and was one of three full-time Hopies who learned to speak it. The children in the hospital loved to have her put them to bed because when she did, she would tell the story of "The Three Little Pigs" in Singalese. When she got to "...and laughed and laughed all the way home", she would tickle the little boy or girl from the foot up to the belly. They loved it, and they loved her. A major local newspaper in Ceylon ran a story about Mary Lou with a photo showing her in uniform and tickling one of the Ceylonese children.

We lived on the ship for that year in a tiny windowless cabin deep inside the vessel. The water in that part of the world is filled with phosphorescent plankton—tiny microorganisms that cannot be seen with the naked eye. But in our totally pitch black cabin, when we flushed the toilet, the bubbling water swirled around the bowl, stirring the phosphorescence of the plankton, and they joined together in a glorious light show as they swirled back into the sea. Our friends would come to our cabin just to watch as we flushed the toilet.

Most of the children we treated were suffering from malnutrition as well as whatever else they were in the hospital for, but some we treated just because they were so severely malnourished.

❧

THE HIDDEN CHILDREN
Ceylon 1967

A child comes to our ship.

His ribs, like the rungs of a ladder,
  climb up his frail chest. He stands, quiet and forlorn.
  His sunken eyes have no interest in this world.
This is malnutrition,
And always present is a heartbreaking apathy.
  Placed in bed, he sits unmoving,
  Without a smile, without a tear,
A child who has learned that nothing, and no one, comes from crying.
Somewhere, behind that wall, a child is hidden.

*With love, with food and with time, glimpses of him may
be seen.*

Cecil holds fiercely to a yellow balloon.
Justin cries if another child has his checkered hat.
Mallika gently rubs her face against a fuzzy animal.
And then more openly — a hesitant, questioning smile —
A small hand is placed in yours,
A child climbs into your lap to be held.

Come out, Cecil. Come out, Mallika and Justin.

Come out, come out, wherever you are. Please come out.

❧

The work in Ceylon was emotionally demanding. Polio had been virtually wiped out in the United States and Europe, but this little island nation had a ninety-bed polio ward at Colombo General Hospital, and it was always filled with children in various stages. We also saw many crippled children suffering the paralytic after-effects.

We wanted to immunize the entire island. It was

possible, but the government of Ceylon opposed us. They wanted to learn more advanced medical techniques such as open-heart surgery, so Bill Walsh arranged for a U.S. cardiac surgical team to come over and work with a Ceylonese cardiac surgical team. The operating conditions of Colombo General Hospital were not good, and the need for open-heart surgery was minimal. Fifteen of the first eighteen cardiac surgical patients died. The children continued to be stricken with polio and paralyzed for life.

Neonatal tetanus was another major problem. Most of the Ceylonese were Buddhists, but many in the north were Hindus who considered the cow to be sacred. A common practice, especially in the rural areas, was to place cow dung on the umbilicus of the newborn baby. Usually within a week, the infant was convulsing with neonatal tetanus. We tried heroically to save three of those infants. They were brought from the countryside by their grief-stricken parents, who usually traveled by bus or train, the infant convulsing periodically throughout the tormented journey. The parents held the S.S. Hope as their only chance.

We started IV's and ran in the antibiotics. We had an anesthesiologist give the anti-convulsant each time the tiny body began another convulsion. We tried to give enough to stop them but not so much that it would kill the infant. We had someone in attendance constantly for each of the three infants we tried to save. We weren't able to save a single one of them.

Ceylon had a tremendous incidence of rheumatic heart disease and glomerulonephritis, especially in children, a rarity in the United States. Both illnesses are due to complications of an infection with streptococcus bacteria. Many of the children had skin rashes oozing with pus. I thought that might account for the rheumatic heart disease. The only way to be sure involved culturing and identifying which strains of strep were involved.

I was able to make an arrangement with the Infectious Disease Center in Atlanta, Georgia, in which I took samples of the skin wounds and in some cases blood cultures, and sent the samples to the Center. They identified the strain of strep involved, and we were able to make the connection between the skin diseases and the rheumatic heart disease. We instituted a simple program for skin care in the children in Colombo that certainly must have lowered the incidence of these diseases.

Once while I was taking a culture from the skin of one of the children, the child jumped, and the needle I was using punctured the palm of my left hand. I finished the culture, put the sample in a test tube and prepared to send it to the Disease Center. I washed my hands.

An hour later, I had a red and swollen area the size of a quarter in my left palm. I took an antibiotic orally. Mary Lou and I were on the deck of the ship when one of the surgeons walked by, and she asked him to look at my hand. He specialized in hand surgery, and knew immediately what he was looking at.

He hospitalized me in the ship's intensive care unit and started an IV with 12 million units of penicillin a day. By the time I was in intensive care unit with the IV started, I was feeling sick and feverish. I don't remember anything of the next three days until I was sitting up in bed and saw Mary Lou and two other nurses holding a tray with a lobster dinner and bottle of white wine. I was lucky.

Others were not as fortunate. One of the physicians aboard the ship had brought his wife and their sixteen-year-old daughter, Leslie, on the mission. One weekend, the surgeon and his wife were away working in another part of the island. Leslie went to the beach with some friends and then returned to the ship.

Eight or ten hours later, someone asked where Leslie was, and we went to her cabin where we found her in bed with a raging fever. She had been swimming at the beach and bacterial contaminated water had gotten into her sinuses. The strain of bacteria was so virulent that it broke through the sinus cavity into her brain and then her bloodstream.

We put her in the intensive care unit and gave her

massive intravenous doses of three different antibiotics, as powerful as available. It was too late. In forty-eight hours, her EKG was a flat line, and a few hours later she was dead.

❧

One of the children who came to the ship was an eleven-year-old girl suffering from heart failure. Our studies led us to the diagnosis of myocarditis, probably viral in origin. We supported her heart as best we could but she was dying. The parents appreciated our efforts but decided to take her off the ship and have her treated by the local Ayervedic doctors. They took her to the mountains where there was a noted healer. We thought she was going to die and doubted that she would survive the trip to the mountain clinic.

She returned with her parents a week later. Her previously pale face was blushed with color. She had left the ship in a wheelchair, but on her return, she ran up the gangplank to see some of her friends on the pediatric ward.

We asked what the doctor had done. They described giving her some potions, a night meeting of the entire village, and prayers and chanting for their daughter. When she had left the ship, we were losing her. They saved her. We examined her after her return and found no evidence of heart disease.

❧

There were other mysteries as well. One of them was the firewalkers. We went to several ceremonies, usually religious, in which a bed of glowing coals had been prepared. The bed was about ten feet wide and forty to fifty feet long. After singing and chanting, the firewalkers would stroll slowly across the glowing bed of coals. We were mystified. Our surgeons were mystified. They asked several of the participants if they would allow small pieces to be taken from their feet. We took the biopsies to our pathology lab, and found no evidence of any damage beyond first-degree burns.

❧

We stayed a little more than a year in Ceylon. We made many friends, not only fellow Hopies but also some of our Ceylonese counterparts. We worked hard. It was emotionally demanding, and we were often exhausted, but we loved what we were doing. Some of the Ceylonese were hostile to us, but I feel that part of our good fortune for many years after was from the good karma that we stored up during that year.

In the year that we were in Ceylon, we explored much of the island. The city of Anuradhapura is fascinating; a sacred city with ruins from earlier cultures. Mary Lou and I stayed on the edge of the jungle, in a hotel built mostly of bamboo. Our room was spacious with a high ceiling. There was a fan slowly turning above us most of the time.

One day in the late afternoon, as we were in our second-story room that faced the jungle, with the sun streaming in through the open windows and cracks in the wall, Mary Lou stepped out of the shower and was standing naked in the middle of the room drying off with a towel.

Suddenly we heard a loud high-pitched cackling

laugh that cackled on and on and on. Mary Lou was startled, wrapped the towel around herself, and turning around in bewilderment, looked out the window to see a three-foot tall gray-haired monkey sitting in a tree and pointing his finger at her. She walked to the window, drew the curtains and yelled, "Stop looking and laughing at me, you dirty old monkey, you!" Then she fell on the bed and couldn't stop laughing. Many times over the years, she would tell me the same thing, "Stop looking and laughing at me, you dirty old monkey, you!"

One of the wonders we had on board was the iron cow, a large machine that made milk, buried in the bowels of the ship. Tom was the wizard of the iron cow. He poured water and mysterious bottles of powder and other things into one end, patiently watched, or occasionally got up and banged other parts of the machine, or cursed at it, and finally collected a stream of milk as it flowed out the other end. We used this on the ship and we gave some to the people of Colombo who would gather at the appointed times for their supply. The opponents to our presence spread the word that the iron cow was a piece of spy equipment used to transmit information to the CIA and FBI.

Tom had another passion—scuba diving. He had brought several scuba tanks along and the other necessary gear, and on days off, he would take several other Hopies out for a dive. The best place to do this was off the coast of Trincomalee, a little village at the opposite end, the northeast end of the island.

Mary Lou and I went with him several times. She became pregnant with Amy while we were on the ship, and the last time we went scuba diving, Mary Lou was about five months pregnant. Tom knew a great deal about the iron cow, but he didn't know much about the scuba diving gear. Sometimes it worked and sometimes it didn't. But we all put on the gear and descended into forty and fifty feet of water.

It was an unbelievably beautiful area. The sun shone deep into the sea. The blue and yellow and gold and red and black and coral striped tropical fish swam before us. In hindsight, we can see how foolish, how dangerous it was to be doing that with inexperienced divers, poor equipment, and guidance from a relative novice. So many things could have happened to Mary Lou and to Amy. We were young and carefree. We were happy and we were foolish. And I believe that God was watching over us.

Mary Lou began to have contractions on the ship on the way back to the United States. She was near term but hardly looked pregnant. The baby was small.

We returned to the United States and went to stay with my parents in New Jersey. Ten days after our return, Mary Lou started having regular contractions, and we went to the hospital.

Amy's birth was a double frank breach. She came out butt first with her legs straight out in front of her and pressed against her chest. This is a very dangerous condition, especially in a woman who has not given birth before. If the labor and delivery had happened on the ship, I don't think Amy, and possibly Mary Lou, would have survived. The condition has a high mortality rate under the best of circumstances.

But Amy waited until we were back in New Jersey and could go to a fully equipped hospital with every possible specialist and piece of equipment needed. After a difficult birth, she and Mary Lou were both fine. Our birth announcements read:

"We brought back a gem from Ceylon—
Amy Lisa Hope Panter
4 lbs. 14 oz.
April 3, 1969."

Connecticut and the Clambake

As a teenager, Mary Lou would occasionally sneak off to see a movie, against the rules of the church, but under the winking eye of her mother. She usually took one or more of her brothers or sisters with her. One of her favorites was *Carousel*. The clambake scene made an especially powerful impression on her. She spoke of it many times. Being born and raised in the flat farmland of lower Michigan probably contributed to her love of this scene and everything connected to it. She was determined to have a clambake.

For the first year of my psychiatric residency at Yale, we lived in an apartment in Hampton just north of New Haven, and definitely part of the city. Mary Lou said we should look for a place near Long Island Sound, which wasn't too far away. We found a small house for rent outside of Guilford, Connecticut, a little east and north of New Haven and near the Sound. The house was in an area called Indian Cove that consisted of fifty homes. Ours was owned and decorated by a man who was the arts editor for an outdoor magazine.

It was perfect for us. We had a five-minute walk to a small beach. The walls of the tiny dining room were lined with weather-beaten barn boards. The candelabra above the dining table held candles only, not electric lights. There was a large backyard with several apple trees, and each spring we saw them burst into bloom.

Mary Lou wanted to have a clambake. I had no idea what was involved, but she knew, either from the movie or from cookbooks. We invited our friends from Yale—my fellow residents, my teachers, our neighbors—and included their kids. A week before the clambake, Mary Lou spent two days digging a rectangular hole in the backyard, eight feet by four feet wide and four feet deep. She really had to work at it because the ground was very hard.

The day before the clambake, she sent me into the woods nearby to bring back enough large stones and rocks to fill half the level of the hole. With a cord of wood that she had bought, Mary Lou built a fire on top of the rocks. We kept it burning for five hours, until the rocks were all hot through and through.

As this was happening, our friends and neighbors were arriving. Nearly a hundred people showed up. As soon as they arrived, there was a job for them. Part of Mary Lou's work ethic was that everybody should help, and everybody had to be kept occupied. Some of our friends kept the fire going and some started husking corn. Others started plucking and preparing chickens.

I took two of my friends with me to the beach and we took a rowboat far out into the Sound until we got to the beds of seaweed. It was very hard work to reach into the water and pull enough seaweed into the boat to nearly fill it. We rowed back to shore and a bunch of the kids came and helped us carry it to the fire.

People had asked if they could bring something. Mary Lou was ready with a list—clams and ears of corn and chickens and soda. The night before the party, I drove an hour up the coast to Old Lyme, Connecticut, and bought two 25-lb. lobsters. They were alive with their claws pegged, but they still looked dangerous. When I got them home, I put them in the bathtub with a little water to keep them alive. I didn't sleep too well that night. I could hear them scratching as they tried to climb the slippery sides, and had visions of them getting out of the tub and grabbing me.

Everyone was busy doing something until we were ready to cook. We took the logs off the rocks and spread a layer of seaweed, then a layer of mussels and clams, then more seaweed, then the corn, more seaweed, then the lobsters, more seaweed, until all the food and seaweed rose a foot or more over the ground. Then we covered it all with a huge tarpaulin.

We all sat back and drank soda and wine. The children played in the backyard, climbing in the trees and tossing a ball for hours, until finally Mary Lou said the food was ready.

Off came the tarpaulin, and the corn was passed around. Off came more seaweed and the chicken was passed around. We uncovered and ate layer by layer, with the lobsters at the end. Have you ever seen a 25-pound lobster? Each was about four feet long! We devoured them, all so delicious.

But we weren't finished. Mary Lou had made apple pies, and some friends brought the ingredients to make ice cream. Anyone with ice cream makers was asked to bring them. We put the ingredients together and packed the ice and salt, and once again, the children were called in to work. They were eager to turn the crank, but after ten or fifteen minutes, each was tired and ready to turn the fun over to the next child. Finally we had pie and ice cream for everyone. For the adults, we had a special topping for the ice cream and there was a story that went with it.

❧

I had become interested in wine making, and after reading books, I bought fermenting jars, bottles and corks, and a corking machine. I made wine out of tomatoes and rhubarb, rose petals and dandelions, and the traditional grapes. Most of it was dreadful, while some of it was at least drinkable, but the grape wine that I made in a five-gallon jar was particularly bad. Hard work had gone into it, though, and I couldn't throw it away, even if it was so bad that we couldn't drink it.

We let it settle more and it was still terrible. One night, our friends Jim and Nicole had invited us to their apartment for dinner. Jim told me to bring my five gallons of wine. His landlord had a bathtub still and he said we could set it up before dinner. While we had a lovely dinner with our friends, the five gallons of terrible wine was distilled down to one gallon of brandy. Eagerly, Jim and I took our tasting sips. The terrible wine had turned into terrible brandy. At least it was easier to handle, as I now only had to take one gallon home.

I still couldn't throw it away, so we let it sit. Just before the clambake, Mary Lou thought of adding some orange flavoring to the brandy, and we did so, hoping that it would taste like Grand Marnier. At the clambake, as the children were devouring their pie à la mode, Mary Lou prepared the ice cream dishes for the adults. She asked me to bring the gallon of brandy into the kitchen. She poured a little of the contents onto a helping of ice cream, handing it to me to sample. I dipped my spoon in and lifted it to my mouth. I swirled it around in my mouth, doing my best imitation of a sommelier at the finest French restaurant. At last! Dreadful brandy from dreadful wine had turned into a fantastic orange-flavored liqueur topping for homemade vanilla ice cream. It was fabulous!

Mary Lou had worked hard for weeks on preparations for that clambake. Our friends came at noon, and we all worked and talked and ate and laughed. When it got dark, the children started to fall asleep on the grass all around the back yard. No one wanted the day to end. I don't think anyone at that clambake will ever forget the day, the party, the aura of friendship and love and happiness. It all started as a vision in the eyes of a Michigan farm girl who stole away for a few hours to see the movie *Carousel*.

❧

Months later, on February 8th, 1971 Mary Lou

and I sat down to dinner at our little table in the dining room. I put some candles in the candelabra and lit them while she finished preparing dinner. Over a leisurely dinner, with Amy sleeping in the next room. We discussed our future. We both loved living in our tiny rented house. Yale was a stimulating exciting university, and although New Haven was a small city, there were plays and concerts and lectures that we went to as often as we could.

We loved living there, but we were in the thirtieth day of a cold spell. The temperature didn't get above thirty degrees for the entire month. We enjoyed the sun and warmth of Southern California—Should we stay in New Haven or return to Southern California?

We made our decision and went to sleep. I remember the date because the next morning, Southern California was hit by the Sylmar Earthquake. When I turned on the television, I saw pictures of the freeways and hospital that had been destroyed. We had experienced smaller earthquakes in Southern California, but we hadn't lived through a big one and didn't know the terror and fear the people

experienced that day. But we had made our deci-
sion.

California

In June, we went to California for a week. Mary Lou was five months pregnant with Adrienne. I interviewed for jobs as a psychiatrist, and we looked for a house to buy. Before leaving New Haven, my cousin had put us in touch with a California attorney who specialized in real estate, and he connected us with a real estate agent. We had written back and forth about what we were looking for and she had a list of properties for us to see.

The first one she took us to was in Sherman Oaks. I liked it and wanted to make an offer. The house was in a lovely neighborhood. It had a rustic feeling yet it was close to the market and other stores. There was a separate area where I could see patients.

Although I wanted to buy it, Mary Lou wanted to see every house on the agent's list, and then even more. We traveled up and down the San Fernando Valley—pregnant Mary Lou with her belly out in front of her, holding Amy in hand, as we looked at living rooms, bedrooms, and pools in Sherman Oaks, Calabasas, Studio City and Woodland Hills. I was exhausted after two days, but Mary Lou wanted to see more, and so we did. Finally she agreed to make an offer on the first house.

My parents offered to give us the down payment. When I was a child we didn't have much money but I never felt poor. My father had gone into business as a gas station owner. He worked hard and believed strongly in customer service.

He saved enough to buy a new car agency in 1939. That was not a good year to go into the automobile business. General Motors, Ford and Chrysler made tanks until 1945. My father worked in the agency during the day and worked the swing shift at the Raritan Arsenal making war materials in the evening. My mother and brother and I hardly ever saw him, but when the war ended and he started getting cars to sell, he began to make good money.

He invested heavily in the stock market, but hated to pay commissions to the broker, so he bought and held. Some were big losers, but he also bought General Electric, Baxter International and other stocks that he just kept. Those went up and split, and up and split, and up again.

I knew nothing of this at the time, but I always had a car to drive. There was also money for as much education as I wanted. And when Mary Lou and I wanted to buy a house, my parents gave us the down payment. I never had to ask my parents for money—other than for medical school—but I always knew that it was there if I needed it.

That was a wonderful safety net. It enabled me to take risks. The payments on the house were more than we could afford on my salary at the Veterans Administration Hospital in Brentwood, but I planned and expected to make enough additional money in part-time private practice to enable us to get by. I never would have reached so high without the safety net of my parents to fall into if needed.

We lived in that house from 1972 until Mary Lou

died. It's a wonderful house. There were several families with children the same ages as ours in the neighborhood. We made many good friends.

All of the kids came to our house, and Mary Lou loved having them. She baked and did arts and crafts and played games and took them to the movies and the park. She always insisted that we buy big cars. Even a station wagon didn't seem big enough. She needed enough room to transport all of the kids and all of the toys. We did very little vactioning in those years.

I worked 7/8 part-time at the VA and started developing a private practice. In a year, I was able to quit the VA. I did everything in general psychiatry—in-patient, outpatient, hospital consultations—and I was very busy.

Mary Lou took care of the children and everything in the house. As a farmer's daughter, she knew a little (and sometimes a lot) about everything. She could do minor plumbing, woodworking, and electrical work, and if we needed to hire someone, she saw to it that the work was done right.

After we lived in our home for several years, I was doing well in my practice, and we were able to send the girls to the private school a few blocks away. Mary Lou became very involved in the school. She worked on the annual fair, donated books, taught special art classes after school, and read stories to the children in the lower grades. She loved it, and the school loved having such a dedicated talented hard worker.

As the girls grew, the pets began to arrive. We had everything—*what ever walked, what ever squawked, what ever swam.* Mary Lou and the children fed chickens, watched the chicks hatch, observed and helped cats and dogs give birth, and took care of the puppies and kittens. They liked to name the pets after food. We had a rabbit named Stew, a cat named Carrots, and a duck named Paté. Our last puppy is Mignon.

The biggest pet we ever had was Shasta, our pony. We didn't live in a pony neighborhood—Our house was in one of the suburbs of Los Angeles. Although our home was set back from the street and we could barely see our neighbors through the trees, the streets were all paved and the homes were next to each other.

Each year, the school nearby held a fair. Mary Lou soon became very active in it. She helped arrange the flowers, set up booths, sell tickets. In whatever area help was needed, she was there. And every year, she brought home something from the auction. One year, it was a painting she liked, and another year, a friend's blueberry pie.

When the girls were six and nine years old, she out-did herself. I was getting into my car in our driveway when I saw her walking down the driveway towards me, leading a pony. I asked her what in the world we would do with a horse. She answered that it was only a pony, and that the girls would love it.

Adrienne's birthday party was coming up and she thought it would be wonderful to give all of the kids pony rides. I thought she meant that we would keep the pony for a few weeks and then get rid of it, but she had other plans. I soon heard other advantages of having a pony, and that the manure would be fabulous for growing the big white asparagus I loved.

The birthday party was a huge success. Having grown up on a farm, Mary Lou had no trouble saddling Shasta up and leading him as eight- and nine and ten-year-olds squealed with delight.

But early one evening she had trouble. Mary Lou was doing something with Shasta—probably watering him—when he pulled back. The rope slipped out of her hand. Shasta ran up the driveway, made a right turn, and started running down the street. Our neighbor was just starting to leave in his Rolls Royce. Mary Lou got to the top of our driveway, hopped into our neighbor's Rolls, and told him to "Follow that pony!"

They drove all over the neighborhood trying to catch Shasta, but every time Mary Lou would get out of the car to grab the halter, Shasta ran through someone's yard and the chase was on again. Soon two police squad cars showed up, and with the help of the police, Shasta was finally corralled. Mary Lou was smiling and telling the policemen how grateful she was for their help, explaining how heart-broken her daughters would be if the pony had truly escaped or gotten hurt.

As she was expressing her great appreciation, one of the police officers was writing out a ticket that he then handed to her.

"Disturbing the peace. Possession of an unlicensed pony in a prohibited area. You are to appear in court on June 12th. If you fail to appear, a warrant for your arrest will be issued."

Mary Lou was shocked. She couldn't believe it. She had grown up with all kinds of animals and never thought about needing a license or having areas that prohibited them.

But on the appointed day, she dressed herself in her sweetest outfit and went to her court appearance. She took a seat and waited and waited in traffic court. When she was finally called and explained what happened, she was told that she was in the wrong court, and to go down the hall to room 312.

When she got to room 312, she took a seat and waited again. This was not what she had expected.

One defendant pleaded guilty to prostitution, the next, "no contest" to burglary. The next was guilty of drug possession. Mary Lou thought there must be some mistake. All she did was have a pony on the loose.

Finally it was her turn to appear before the judge. He looked so somber and forbidding, and he'd been handing out very stiff sentences—jail for six months, a thousand-dollar fine, no possibility of bail. Mary Lou was scared.

The bailiff read the charges. "Illegal possession of a pony in a restricted neighborhood. Failure to have a license. Disturbance of the peace."

The judge listened and put on his sternest look. He asked the police officer about the "disturbance of the peace" charge. As the policeman was explaining what happened with the escaped pony and about the chase in the Rolls Royce and running through back yards, Mary Lou was interrupting with her explanations. The judge began to smile and then couldn't hold back his laughter, and he was joined by most of the drug addicts, prostitutes and burglars in the court—her fellow defendants.

The judge pulled himself together, stared down at Mary Lou, and told her in his sternest, most somber tone that these were very serious charges. He asked her how she wanted to plead. Mary Lou replied in her sweetest most charming voice, "No contest, your Honor."

He dismissed all of the charges against her but warned that he didn't want to see her in his courtroom again, or he wouldn't be so lenient the next time. She thanked him and said that we would get rid of the pony.

Amy and Adrienne were heartbroken, but Shasta had to go. The school fair was coming up again in a few weeks, and Mary Lou donated Shasta back to the fair. Another lucky family became the proud owners of our pony.

❧

Mary Lou's love of reading was a gift she shared with our children. Every night there was a story— *Winnie the Pooh, Tom Sawyer, Huckleberry Finn,*

Tigger the Tiger. They heard them all. And from the time our girls were three and four years old, Mary Lou started taking them on adventures. They panned for gold in Placerita Canyon. They went to the ghost town of Calico, to Disneyland and Raging Waters. How could Erma have known that letting her little girl escape behind the barn with a book would lead to a lifelong love of reading, of learning, of traveling and seeking adventure? But it did, and my life and the lives of our children and many friends have been richer for it.

The difference in our religions was never a problem, never even an issue—We celebrated everything. Hanukkah parties and Passover Seders were spent at the homes of my parents and cousins, and Christmas took over our own home.

Mary Lou was ecstatic about Christmas. She started her annual frenzy about a month before. There was a present for everyone and often two or three or four. When she was a child, Christmas meant looking at the Sears catalog, dreaming of all the wonderful possibilities, and receiving one very inexpensive present. After we married, she overdid it a bit to compensate. The children and I tried to calm her down, but she had such energy and drive and love that we were not very successful.

She made Christmas baskets for many of our friends and family members. Each basket had one of her rum cakes, one of her pecan pies, bottles of red and white wines and cognac, candy and fruits. It was so much work, but she so dearly loved doing it.

Sometimes a friend or someone in the family would worry that our children were confused about their religious identities, but I don't think they were. When Adrienne was four years old, someone asked her what religion she was. Her answer was the best I've ever heard for children of a mixed marriage, "I am Jewish and Christmas."

Traveling Again and the Conferences

Our longest vacation for the first seven or eight years in California was a three-day weekend at the Holiday Inn on the beach in Ventura, about an hour's drive north of our home.

In 1978, we took our first big vacation, a week in Hawaii at Christmas. We loved it and the travel bug bit us again. We took the girls skiing at Sun Valley, and then in 1980, we spent four weeks in Europe together with my mother. We rented a car and traveled as Mary Lou and I had on our honeymoon, with no reservations or planned route. We just went wherever we wanted to go, stayed as long as we wanted to, and then went on to the next city. The first summer we vacationed for four weeks, and the second for five.

There were many reasons we were compelled to visit Amsterdam. I have been reading books and articles about Vincent van Gogh for many years, and wanted to see his work in the Van Gogh Museum and the Kroller-Muller Museum in Otterloo, an hour's drive from the city. The Van Gogh Museum is a fantastic chronologically arranged museum of many of his greatest and best-known works.

I loved it, but the girls were less than thrilled. They wanted to play, so we went to the Kroller-Muller Museum, which is in a national park. Admission includes free use of the many white bicycles that were parked everywhere. Once we drove in and left our car, the girls wanted to ride, so the four of us got on the bikes. For an hour and a half, we peddled over the narrow paved bicycle paths through the green rolling countryside surrounding the museum. It was a slightly overcast misty day. The sun occasionally shone through the clouds and flashed on the leaves as we peddled by. It was a magical afternoon.

When the girls were tired, they plopped themselves down on the soft cushions of the benches in the front of the museum, and Mary Lou and I went to look at Vincent's paintings. "The Cut Sunflowers", "Pere Tanquay", "The Postman Roulin", "Starry Night". I was thrilled. I had read about and studied these paintings, and to see them altogether was stunning.

As we were going through the museum, we met Fritz, a fellow about our age, perhaps a little younger. He was an American, married to a Dutch girl, and worked as a tour guide in Holland. On this day, he was on vacation. As we walked with him from painting to painting, talking and getting to know each other, sharing pieces of our lives, we realized that he knew a tremendous amount about the artist and the paintings. We were together for about two hours and that time greatly enhanced my knowledge and understanding of van Gogh.

We exchanged names and phone numbers. Years later when Mary Lou and I did our first conference in Europe—in Amsterdam, Brussels, Paris and Cannes—I contacted Fritz, and he organized everything for us in Holland. He escorted a group through the Van Gogh Museum and once again through the Kroller-Muller Museum. I'm still in touch with him, and every time I go to Amsterdam, we get together.

While in Amsterdam, we wanted the girls to see the Anne Frank House. We left our hotel, map in hand, and found our way to the small museum. We went through it in about an hour. Mary Lou and I were very moved by it, as were the girls. They could identify with the little Jewish girl in hiding and with her story.

As we left the house, I wanted to take a picture of Amy, Adrienne and Mary Lou in front of it. I asked them to pose. I backed off to compose the picture, kneeling down for a better angle. I didn't notice, but the girls did, that as I knelt, I put my right knee into a small pile of dog poop. Amy and Adrienne squealed with delight. I asked what was going on. They said, "Daddy, watch it." Then I said, "Watch shit." Then Mary Lou said, "Wash it." "Whooaa shit." "What shit!" We have found many variations of the words over the years, and the girls still occasionally say with a wink, "Daddy, watch it."

My mother suffered from episodes of depression followed by euphoria. We all enjoy her episodes of hypomania. During one of those summers in Europe, she was feeling great. The streets of Interlaken were lined with jewelry stores and their windows displayed beautiful bracelets and necklaces and clothes, and of course, a wonderful array of watches.

As we walked down the street, I stopped to look in one of the windows. My mother came up and asked if I saw anything that I liked. I had been looking at a gold Omega watch with a band designed as a gold bracelet. I pointed it out to her and then we continued down the street.

That night at dinner, she said she wanted to show me what she had bought that day. I thought she was going to pull out a hat or a scarf or one of the things I'd seen her admiring, but out came the gold Omega and she gave it to me. I was surprised and pleased. And then out came another box—the exact same watch. She said she liked it so much that she bought one for my father. He wore his watch until he died. Now it belongs to David. I've been wearing mine for over twenty-five years. A good luck charm? A wonderful timepiece? My mother's love and happiness are always with me upon my wrist.

❧

I think it's impossible to walk across the Ponte Vecchio of Florence without buying a ring or a wallet. If you do and the authorities find out, they probably won't stamp your passport, and you won't be allowed to leave the country. Mary Lou and I stopped at one of the stalls and she bought a green glass ring for $12 and gave it to my mother. When her friends asked where she got "that beautiful emerald ring" or comment on how expensive it must have been, my mother just smiled and said that it was a gift from Mary Lou. She loved wearing that ring, and of course, it wasn't about a piece of jewelry.

❧

Some of Mary Lou's ancestors had lived in Alsace-

Lorraine, so of course, we had to visit the area. We saw the cathedral in Mulhouse, and we drove along the wine road, spending several nights at a lovely auberge in Ribersville.

The highlight of our trip was to be dinner at the three-star Auberge de l'Ille. My mother had volunteered to stay with the girls in our little hotel. Mary Lou and I dressed for dinner and got into our rented car. I noticed that we were low on gas so I stopped at the first gas station we saw. I filled the tank and off we went.

About two kilometers down the road, the car made a very loud belching sound and I saw a huge black cloud emerge from the tailpipe. Soon the car began sputtering. I pulled it to the side of the road before it came to a halt. I looked under the hood and found nothing wrong. The gendarmes arrived and asked if we needed help. They called a gas station in the nearby town and a driver arrived with his tow truck. He loaded the car onto his truck with us in the car, and took us to his station which was in back of his home.

He had soon diagnosed the problem as diesel fuel

in the tank instead of gasoline. He said that he would have to lift the car and drain the tank. I told him about our dinner reservations and asked how long it would take. He apologized and said it would take several hours. I felt terrible. Mary Lou and I had looked forward to the dinner for a long time.

The owner of the gas station saw that we were disappointed and asked us if we would like to eat with his wife and their two children while he worked on the car. We gratefully accepted. She began working in the kitchen, and when she started to peel potatoes, Mary Lou asked if she could help. Soon both of them were happily working, arranging dishes on the table, and placing glasses and bread. When dinner was ready, Mary Lou and I sat with her and the children, and her husband came and joined us. The children told us about their school, and we told them about our children who were about the same age. We talked about schools in the United States, and told them how much we loved France. We had a delightful dinner with a charming French family.

In several hours, our car was ready. As we were

driving back to the hotel, I apologized to Mary Lou and told her that I still owed her a dinner at Auberge de l'Ille She chided me and said she couldn't imagine a more wonderful evening than the one we had with that gracious family. Over the years, we talked about going to the restaurant, but we never did. Mary Lou said that if we ever returned to Alsace-Lorraine, she wanted me to fill the car with diesel so that we could have dinner with that family again.

❧

In the winter of '80-'81, we planned to go skiing again, this time to Snowmass, but to our amazement, Mary Lou was pregnant!

We had tried to have a third child, and after several years without success, we went to a fertility specialist. Tests were done, with no conclusions. The next test would have been invasive—He wanted to do a laparoscopic examination of the abdomen to get a good look at Mary Lou's ovaries, fallopian tubes and uterus. We decided not to do it, and forgot about another child. Nine years later, Mary Lou was pregnant with David.

I think the reason she was able to finally get pregnant was because her internist, Ed Shulkin, made the diagnosis of mild hypothyroidism and put her on thyroid. It's incredible and makes me angry to think that the fertility specialist put us through so many tests and procedures and didn't do the simple blood test to diagnose hypothyroidism.

We were delighted with the news but had to cancel the ski plans. I made arrangements for us to go to Maui, and later read that there was to be a medical meeting at the same time—two actually. I had a choice of "Pain" or "Antibiotics". I wasn't into pain so I decided to attend the meeting on antibiotics.

On the first day of the conference, I walked out of the brilliant sunlight in paradise into a darkened room and soon was looking at pictures of bacteria on the screen. I wanted to scream it was so boring! I was angry—Why didn't someone put on a conference that was more interesting, more fun—

a conference that a spouse could go to and enjoy, where a couple could sit around the pool in the afternoon and at dinner that night and discuss what they'd heard that morning?

No one was doing anything like that. Mary Lou listened to my complaints and heard my anger. She let me cool down and then suggested that I put on such a conference. I told her I didn't know the first thing about doing one, but she pointed out that I had just told her in detail what would work. I argued that I would have to find a hotel, put together a program, get speakers. She said we should do it.

I thought about it—What would the conference be about? What flashed into my mind immediately was the psychological studies of art and artists.

During my training to become a psychoanalyst, I was required to analyze three patients under supervision. I was very fortunate with my first analysand, a young woman artist. My supervisor, Rudy Ekstein is a warm and wonderful human being, and I am grateful to both of them for what

I learned during the three and a half years of her analysis.

She told me her dreams and associated freely to them and to all of her thoughts and feelings. She painted many pictures during those years. Many were self-portraits. As each was finished, she brought the painting to the office for me to look at, but didn't want me to talk about it and didn't want to talk about it herself. We didn't, but in discussing her dreams and her associations and learning so much about her, I saw her paintings in a way I had never seen art before. I could see so much of what she was telling me there on her canvases.

Another requirement for graduation from the psychoanalytic institute was to write a paper. Mine was "Portraits of a Psyche", about this patient and her paintings. A member of the Institute was putting a program together on "The Psychopathology of the Artist" for the UCLA extension division. He had read my paper in the institute library and asked me to be part of his program. I told him I wanted to do it but I couldn't present "Portraits of the Psyche" because the paintings were too revealing, and it would have been a breach of confidentiality. It would have been unfair and unkind to my patient.

I offered to present another artist—Vincent van Gogh. Mary Lou helped me do the research and we poured over books about him. We looked at his paintings and discussed them. Mary Lou loved to read and when she got her teeth into something, she wouldn't let go until she had had a good bite of it. I wrote the paper and presented it at UCLA, "Vincent van Gogh—A Study of Creativity and Madness".

Many people who study van Gogh also become interested in Paul Gauguin. Soon Mary Lou and I were researching his life for another paper. I was looking for an emotionally healthy artist to counter the unsound Vincent, so we studied the life of Marc Chagall. I titled my paper, "Marc Chagall—Creativity and Emotional Growth". The subject for our conference was right in front of us—"Creativity and Madness: Psychological Studies of Arts and Artists".

I knew other psychiatrists and psychologists with

similar interests and asked them to be part of our conference. Soon the program was complete, but I needed a place to hold it.

The conference I had attended on antibiotics was during Easter week at the Hyatt Regency on the Kaanapali Coast of Maui. I called the hotel and told them I would like to reserve a block of rooms and meeting space for an Easter week conference. They looked at their reservations and told me they would be happy to host the conference—in five years.

I contacted other hotels and received the same answer. A Marriott Hotel was under construction on Maui. I called and asked them about availability. They were delighted and gracious and welcoming. Our conference was planned for the second week of April 1982. I was assured that the hotel would be finished no later than mid-March.

Being incredibly naive, I signed the contract and put together a brochure and mailed it out in September of 1981. By the end of November, only five people had registered. The hotel called to ask how things were going and to remind me that a very large deposit was due in ten days.

We were in a quandary. Should we cut our losses—the money we had spent printing and mailing the brochure and an initial deposit—and call it quits, or should we pay the $15,000 and hope that more people would register? We had so much of ourselves invested in the effort that we couldn't abandon it, even if it meant we'd lose more money. I gave them the deposit. In the next three or four months, it looked like enough people would attend that we'd lose only a little money.

Then another problem arose—The hotel called to inform me that because of winter storms, construction was delayed and they weren't sure the hotel would be open in time for our conference. They had inquired if other hotels in the area could host our meeting, but there were no rooms available anywhere. They apologized and said they would keep me posted.

We worried and waited and hoped. The Marriott assured us that they would refund the money, but we had also given deposits to the airlines to hold seats, and they would not offer refunds. The people who had registered were looking forward to a week on Maui and to our conference.

The hotel made it. It opened one week before our conference! Enough people had registered that we only lost a little money. Those who attended the conference loved it, and told us that they had never been to anything like it before. Mary Lou and I, Amy and Adrienne and David (in a stroller most of the time at six months of age) all had a wonderful week. When it was finished and we had returned home, I went into PCD—post-conference depression. Mary Lou suggested that we do it again the following year. It was a great idea and that's how our conference business began.

Love

She gave me what I needed. Her love nourished and healed my wounded soul.

I think I gave Mary Lou much of what she needed. Many of her wishes to "travel beyond my ken" were fulfilled. I adored her, and gave her everything I thought she wanted that was within our means.

She had trouble spending money on herself. I wanted her to buy finer clothes, and occasionally she would or I would buy something for her, but she usually bought less expensive things from catalogs. Having grown up so poor—having put the needs of others before hers—it was hard to spend on herself, but her beauty and taste were such that she could wear anything and look good in it.

I fell head over heels in love with you

The moment I first saw you.
And I have loved you ever since.

Was our love a constant? Yes, it was. Were there fluctuations in our love? Yes, of course. In the beginning, I was infatuated with her. Everything about her was wonderful and perfect. Her family had the idyllic farm life—Everyone was happy and working and helping each other. As I got to know the family better, I saw the flaws.

For a number of years I felt that after the initial infatuation, I was the stronger and that I did more for our family than she did. The last seven or eight years of our marriage, I began to realize more and more with each passing year, how remarkable she was, and how fortunate I was and our children were.

Her faults? Of course she had faults, but they were more the self-destructive kind than those that could hurt someone else. If there are angels walking this earth, then Mary Lou surely was one of them—just as I believe the nurses and aides who cared for her during her long hospital stay would also be counted among them. She shared a wonderful bond with them. They were sisters in angelhood.

I felt then as I do now that she gave far more to our love and marriage than I did, that I was far more fortunate in marrying her than she was in marrying me. She told me that although she knew in her heart that I loved her, she felt that she loved me more. If there must be an argument in a marriage, let it be about this. I felt at times she was right, but toward the end I can't imagine anyone loving someone more than I loved her.

So these poems and this book are the natural, almost effortless outpouring of my love for her.

Several weeks after Mary Lou entered the hospital, the poems started to come to me, sometimes while I was in the hospital at her side, and other times sitting at home listening to Pachelbel or Puccini, or looking at her photo. I wrote them down on whatever scrap of paper was at hand, and then put them into the computer. After several months, I wondered how many there were. The number was six or seven. I thought it would be appropriate if there were thirty-three, one for every year of our marriage. The poems continued to come. As they did, I wrote them down and read them to her in the hospital. She loved them and wanted to have them with her, so I printed each one on a five-inch square card, laminated it, and gave it to her. She often fell asleep holding one in her hands.

They kept coming until about a month after she died. I remember thinking—almost being jolted by the awareness—There had been no poems in more than a month. I wondered how many there were and counted—there were thirty-three.

The September following Mary Lou's death, Adrienne and Amy and I went to London and Stratford-on-Avon for one of our conferences. I saw seven shows in two-and-a-half weeks. I'd forgotten how thrilling the London stage is. I saw lavishly produced musicals, *Henry the Fifth* by the Royal Shakespeare Company in Stratford and several wonderful shows with only three actors. As I was sitting in the theater watching *Art*, the idea came to me of using *Thirty-Three Poems for Mary Lou* as the starting point of a play. I worked on it for several months, but ran into obstacles. The only thing I know about playwriting is what I have observed seeing plays over the years. The chances of having a play produced are not good. I decided to write this book instead, but would like to end with what I envisioned as the final scene of the play.

Mary Lou's coffin is lowered into the ground as the family and friends surround the gravesite.

A yellow rose upon your casket
slowly slowly into the ground.
My heart goes with you.
My heart goes with you, Darling,
into the grave.

I close my eyes once more and see before me on a stage—myself, my children, our friends—around Mary Lou's waiting grave. I place a yellow rose, her favorite, upon her casket. The stage darkens as it goes slowly, slowly into the ground. From above, yellow petals start to fall, slowly at first, glittering against the darkness, glittering as the light reflects against them as they fall, then more and more until they cover the shoulders of all of us standing there, and more and more as they cover the grave.

Then Mary Lou steps out of the darkness, out of her grave.

Erma steps out of the shadows and takes her hand:

> "Mary Lou, my darling daughter. You were always such a help to me. I love you Mary Lou. I love you."

"Mama. You put your dreams into me. You read to me. You made me dream of adventures. You led me to the road and pushed me forward so I could see the world. I love you, Mama."

Jesse steps forward:

> "My first born, my baby girl. I'm sorry I made you so angry. I'm sorry I hurt you. I'm sorry I hurt the boys."

"I understand, Papa. You worked so hard for all of us. I love you, Papa."

Stanley takes her hand:
> "You were more like a mother to me
> than a sister. I always felt so safe and
> loved whenever you were with me."

"I love you, Stanley. I've always loved you."

Amy, Adrienne, David:
> "Oh, Mama, the adventures you took us
> on! You made everything so exciting.
> Everything was fun when we were with
> you. I love you. I love you."

*"I loved every moment of loving you. I loved
bathing you, and singing to you, and combing
your hair, and taking you on adventures. You
filled my heart with joy. I love you. I love you."*

Barry:

"Sweetheart, you healed my heart. You nourished my soul. I tried to give you the world. I only wish I could have made all of your dreams come true."

"Oh, my darling, you made so many of them come true. I rode with the riders of the purple sage. I traveled around the world. I went beyond my ken."

"Yes, but you had other dreams...."

"And if all my dreams had come true, what would that mean? Only that my dreams weren't big enough."

"I love you, Mary Lou. I loved you from the moment I first saw you. I will always love you."

"And I love you, with all my heart. You are my heart's true desire. I love you. I will always love you."

Everyone, all the voices as in a fugue, reaching hands out to each other and to everyone:

"I love you. I love you. There is only love here. There is no more powerful force in all the world. Love to you. I love you. Love to you. I love you."

Epilogue

As I sit on the beach...

I see a man walking by backwards as he takes a video of his five-year-old daughter...a couple in their forties holding hands...three teenage girls giggling...there he goes, a twenty-five-year old jogging by. Here come two boys about ten. Life is parading in front of me.

I see a father yelling at his son. I see a mother angrily grab her little girl's arm. I silently say to them—Don't you know? Don't you realize how fortunate you are? Don't you understand? Cherish these moments. Cherish these years. You are together. You are healthy. You have so much before you. Love each other—just love each other....

A man in his thirties, carrying his three-year-old on his shoulders. Another couple holding hands.

They just stopped, looked at the sunset and kissed, then continued their walk...I see a young couple facing each other, arms around each other's waist...and I smile. They know.

It's love—that is all that is really of value, all that we really have to give to each other. It's love that gives us happiness.

᠅ ᠅ ᠅

Twenty-one months

I felt your hand upon my shoulder
holding me at first.
and then—
a gentle push
your loving touch

It's all right
it's time
move on...